"I'm upside down or something—I can't ah . . .
"I'm not spinning now—but I'm . . .
"I'm not spinning but . . .
"I can't seem [unintelligible]. *I can't seem to get*
my [unintelligible]."

The transmission ended abruptly.

Search and rescue efforts over Lake Erie were
launched immediately. Search craft were directed
by Cleveland Center to the precise location of the
disappearance. No trace of the plane or its four
passengers were found. Not a scrap of wreckage
located.

———————

The *Bannockburn* was a sturdy steel ship carrying grain on Lake Superior. Captain James
McMaugh of the *Algonquin* was bound on roughly
the opposite course. The *Bannockburn* must have
been a majestic sight on this fine day because
Captain McMaugh called to his mate to point her
out. But McMaugh's remark caused some confusion in the *Algonquin* pilot house. The *Bannockburn* was no longer there.

The *Bannockburn* had disappeared forever!

———————

HOW AND WHY DO THESE THINGS HAP-
PEN?

DOES SOMEONE KNOW?

PERHAPS.

THE
GREAT LAKES
TRIANGLE

Jay Gourley

A FAWCETT GOLD MEDAL BOOK

Fawcett Publications, Inc., Greenwich, Connecticut

Grateful acknowledgment is made to the authors and publishers for permission to reprint:

From *Aliens from Space* by Donald E. Keyhoe. Copyright © 1973 by Donald E. Keyhoe. Reprinted by permission of Doubleday & Company, Inc. and Panther Books of Granada Publishing Limited.

From *The Bermuda Triangle* by Charles Berlitz. Copyright © 1974 by Charles Berlitz. Reprinted by permission of Doubleday & Company, Inc. and Souvenir Press of London.

From *The UFO Experience: A Scientific Inquiry* by J. Allen Hynek. Copyright © 1972 by J. Allen Hynek. Reprinted by permission of Henry Regnery Company.

From *The Edge of Reality* by J. Allen Hynek and Jacques Vallee. Copyright © 1975. Reprinted by permission of Henry Regnery Company.

From *Ghost Ships of the Great Lakes* by Dwight Boyer. Copyright © 1968. Reprinted by permission of Dodd, Mead & Company, Inc.

From *Great Stories of The Great Lakes* by Dwight Boyer. Copyright © 1966. Reprinted by permission of Dodd, Mead & Company, Inc.

From *Inland Seas*. Copyright © 1961. Reprinted by permission of *Inland Seas*, a quarterly journal of the Great Lakes Historical Society, Volume 17, pages 94-96.

THE GREAT LAKES TRIANGLE

ISBN 0-449-13827-5

Printed in the United States of America

10 9 8 7 6 5 4 3 2 1

Contents

INTRODUCTION

There exists within the United States and Canada—
principally between longitudes 76° west and 92° west and
between latitudes 41° north and 49° north—a region in
which several hundred peculiar events have been recorded.
The concentration of such events is far greater than any
random statistical dispersion would place within these
narrow boundaries.

The region, on the whole, is sparsely populated, but
there are areas of dense population within it.

The principal geographic features of this region are
five freshwater lakes.

Chapter One:

THE QUESTION

In 1950, as today, aircraft flying blind through the clouds reported passing certain checkpoints. Ordinarily the pilot notified Air Traffic Control of the time he crossed the reporting point, his estimated time of arrival at the next reporting point and his altitude. For instance, a typical position report would be: "Northwest 2501, Battle Creek at 51 [minutes past the hour]. Estimating Milwaukee at 37. Level 3500 [feet above mean sea level]." With that information Air Traffic Control could monitor the flight's progress and keep it separated from other aircraft. On June 23, 1950, Northwest Airlines Flight 2501[1] made just such a report at 37 minutes past the hour of 11:00 P.M. as it crossed the radio navigation fix that defined Battle Creek, Mich.

Northwest 2501 was westbound out of New York City's La Guardia Airport headed for Seattle, Wash. Flying the DC-4 was Capt. Robert C. Lind. To his right was co-pilot Verne F. Wolfe. In the passenger section were stewardess Bonnie A. Feldman and 55 passengers. The passenger manifest included the wife of a vice president of General Mills, the vice president of International Telephone and Telegraph and his family, the associate editor of Ideal Publishing Co., a sportswear manufacturer's representative, the research director of New York City's Budget Commission, and a priest. The airplane carried 2500 gallons of fuel. From Lind's estimated time en route between Battle Creek and Milwaukee, we may conclude that he was calculating his groundspeed at something just over 185 knots, or a little faster than 210 miles per hour. But an estimate is just that. It is quite ordinary for an airplane to run two or three minutes ahead of or behind its pilot's estimate.

Lind's estimate proved to be exceptionally inaccurate. It has been more than 26 years, and Northwest 2501 has yet to report crossing Milwaukee.

Northwest 2501's delay brought national attention for several days. It was, according to newspaper reports of the time, "the nation's worst aviation disaster."

At sunrise on June 24, 1950, the United States Coast Guard began what soon became one of the most extensive searches in the history of Lake Michigan. Experts knew that if Northwest 2501 had exploded in flight the Coast Guard would find Lake Michigan covered with wreckage. This was likely, since Captain Lind had not radioed a distress call. If Lind had landed the airplane intact, rescuers would find it floating on the surface or resting on the bottom. They might find survivors.

What they found was the aircraft logbook floating mysteriously on the surface of Lake Michigan 18 nautical miles north-northwest of Benton Harbor, Mich.

With persistence, the Coast Guard scoured the bottom of Lake Michigan. Later the Navy sent its most sophisticated anti-submarine experts to find this huge submerged metallic object. There was little doubt that they would ultimately succeed. "Investigators were confident last night that wreckage of a missing Northwest Airlines' DC-4 plane was at the bottom of Lake Michigan from three to five miles off shore between St. Joseph, Mich., and South Haven, 32 miles north," according to *The Chicago Tribune.* "Secret Navy radar and sonar devices will be used to sweep the lake bottom."

The remains of Northwest 2501 were never found.

The Civil Aeronautics Board investigators pored over every clue. They interviewed the Civil Aviation Administration's air traffic controllers. They investigated the life histories of Northwest 2501's crew as well as the history of the DC-4 itself. Little came of this exhaustive inquiry beyond what was apparent by sunrise on June 24, 1950: Somewhere over Lake Michigan, something had altered the course of events planned by Captain Lind.

The next year the Civil Aeronautics Board finally made

9

its report on the "probable cause" of the accident. In this case it was one of the shortest and most unusual of such reports ever recorded for a major airline disaster. It said, "The Board determines that there is not sufficient evidence upon which to make a determination of probable cause." It was signed by the three board members who had supervised the massive investigation.

Aside from the strange disappearance of the plane itself, the most serious problem facing investigators was the absence of vast wreckage on the surface of Lake Michigan. It was not consistent with Captain Lind's failure to transmit a distress signal. "None of the radio communications received from the flight, including the last, contained any mention of trouble," reported the board. At the same time, the "possibility that this accident resulted from some mechanical failure seems to be remote . . ."

About an hour after Northwest 2501 was due in Milwaukee, two policemen in a Milwaukee suburb saw a glimmering red light floating high above Lake Michigan to the east-southeast—toward Battle Creek. It was not an aircraft. The two officers had worked nights regularly. They had never seen anything like it before. They had no idea that one of history's worst aviation disasters was in the making.

No one knows what this twinkling red light over Lake Michigan was. (See Chapter Three)

When Hull No. 301 was launched as the *Edmund Fitzgerald*[2] she was the largest vessel on the Great Lakes. More than 700 feet long, 75 feet wide and 39 feet deep, she had a capacity greater than 26,000 tons. She was a mammoth structure. On February 19, 1975, her hull was inspected by the Coast Guard. It was in good condition. Her lifesaving gear was checked on March 19, 1975. It, too, was in good condition.

On November 9, 1975, the *Edmund Fitzgerald* was loaded with 26,216 tons of taconite pellets—a kind of refined iron ore. This taconite was from the Burlington-Northern dock in Duluth, Minn. It was 1:15 P.M. when Capt. Ernest R. McSorley, a veteran of 44 years of Great

10

Lakes sailing, guided the *Edmund Fitzgerald* out of Duluth-Superior Harbor. Seas were quiet. Over the next 24 hours a moderate storm developed over Lake Superior. It caused minor damage to the railing and vents on the *Fitzgerald*. At 3:30 P.M. Captain McSorley mentioned the damage in a radio-telephone conversation with Capt. Jesse B. Cooper, master of the nearby *Arthur M. Anderson*. The *Arthur M. Anderson* and the *Fitzgerald* were traveling in tandem, the *Fitzgerald* leading toward the locks that would lower them to the level of Lake Huron, still 100 miles away.

Traveling together provided each of these ships with an added measure of safety. The *Fitzgerald* was about 17 miles ahead of the *Anderson* that afternoon, but the *Fitzgerald* checked her speed so that the *Anderson* could close that distance. Captain Cooper later recalled that Captain McSorley "gave no indication that he was worried or that he had a problem or there was something he couldn't cope with. There was no excitement or whatever. This is what you would assume from the way he talked, that there was no problem." Just before 7:30 P.M., Captain Cooper returned to the *Anderson's* pilot house. The *Anderson's* mate had just talked with the *Fitzgerald*. The *Fitzgerald* was about nine miles ahead according to the *Anderson's* radar.

At sea, waves reflect radar. This "sea return" shows as a bright spot in the center of the circular radar screen. The strength of the sea return varies, but on November 10, 1975, the *Anderson's* radar display was painting sea return over everything within nine miles of the ship. Consequently, when the *Fitzgerald* faded into the obscuring sea return, Captain Cooper knew only that he was within nine miles of the *Fitzgerald*, and that the distance was diminishing. For a few minutes he could not see the *Fitzgerald* because a snow flurry restricted his visibility. That was just a few minutes. Then the snow lifted. Captain Cooper could see for 20 miles.

There was no *Fitzgerald*.

This was extraordinary, but Captain Cooper had not fully realized how really strange it was when he first contacted the Coast Guard just before 8:00 P.M., November

10, 1975. "I informed them of my concern over the *Fitzgerald*, that I thought she had floundered," he said. Upon later reflection Captain Cooper described scornfully how "they reported to *me* to be on the lookout for a 16-foot boat that was lost in Whitefish Bay." Cooper was angry at the Coast Guard for dismissing his fears so lightly, but he understood. "I think they were like I was. I don't think they could believe a ship could go down that fast . . ." After all, if the *Fitzgerald* had been in trouble, why hadn't the *Fitzgerald* reported it? The *Fitzgerald* had radios backed up by more radios—all designed for even the most improbable contingencies. The flip of a switch would activate automatic battery-powered distress signals on several frequencies. There is nothing that can happen to a ship the size of the *Fitzgerald* so quickly that there is not time to flip a switch. No such transmissions were ever made. Therefore it was impossible for the *Fitzgerald* to have sunk as Captain Cooper was suggesting.

Yet there stood Captain Cooper, looking out across the blank face of Lake Superior, with no *Fitzgerald* to be seen. Cooper radioed other ships nearby and asked if they could see or paint a radar echo from the *Fitzgerald*. They could not. Cooper knew the Coast Guard would not believe him. "When I called the second time, I said, 'I *know* she is down,'" Cooper later recalled.

He was right.

Eventually a few liferafts and lifeboats were found. There was no evidence they had been launched. Apparently they were torn free by whatever incomprehensible force was strong enough to pull a 26,000-ton freighter instantly to her death. A man in a lifejacket on one of these lakes, though he may be dead of exposure, is inevitably found. No one from the *Fitzgerald* has been found.

This is consistent with the other curious facts of the disaster. Apparently, even the crewmen on duty at the time of the accident failed to put on their lifejackets and step outside the pilot house—a procedure that would require no more than 10 or 15 seconds.

Whatever fate befell the *Fitzgerald*, it struck with such

speed that her crew lacked even the time to be afraid.

Just a few hours after the *Fitzgerald* vanished, a seemingly unrelated but equally curious drama began to unfold in the Canadian skies a few miles east of where the *Fitzgerald* vanished. That event is described in Chapter Three.

Compared to the incidents themselves, it may not seem particularly odd that the total disappearance of Northwest 2501 and the mysteriously rapid destruction of the *Edmund Fitzgerald* occurred in such proximity. Something unusual happens almost everywhere at some time or another. What defies reason is that the *Edmund Fitzgerald* and Northwest 2501 are perfectly typical of hundreds and possibly thousands of equally curious events that seem concentrated in, over and around these lakes.

As an aviator-turned-journalist I have spent much time examining federal aviation accident investigation files—now under the jurisdiction of the National Transportation Safety Board. Out of personal and professional curiosity I frequently browse through the "missing aircraft unrecovered" files at the board's headquarters in Washington, D.C. These are the mystery files—the accidents that stimulate one's imagination. It was early in 1975 that I first noticed an unusual concentration of reports involving aircraft overflying the Great Lakes. I asked whether there was a pattern, and was advised to talk to a National Transportation Safety Board statistician, computer expert and information specialist named Starke Jett. Several months before, Jett had noticed the same pattern. He already had done a statistical analysis to satisfy his own curiosity. He had found that the Great Lakes accounted for more of these strange accidents than the famous Bermuda Triangle. He offered no reason, but confirmed that there is an incredible concentration of "missing aircraft unrecovered" that, from all available information, disappeared near the Great Lakes. He compared it to the Bermuda Triangle, but laughed at the notion that the cause was anything beyond current scientific principles.

Intrigued by Jett's conclusions, I made my own statistical analysis of ten sample years of accidents in this file. The result: The Bermuda Triangle and the Great Lakes dominate the face of the earth in any geographical comparison of U.S.-registered civil aircraft that "fly away."[3]

Then I noticed a peculiar feature of these strange disappearances. Many could not be explained by the government investigators who studied them. For most missing aircraft there is at least some hint of a cause—a radio distress call, a scrap of wreckage, a witness, an odd position report, a severe meteorological condition or a calculable fuel shortage. But all too often among these accidents there was nothing. And when there was evidence, it was almost characteristically confusing and contradictory.

I checked comparable files at the Canada Department of Transport, Ottawa, Ont. The same conclusion held, except that for Canadian-registered civil aircraft, not even the Bermuda Triangle has compared to the Great Lakes.

I talked to Rear Adm. J. S. Gracey of the United States Coast Guard Ninth District headquarters, Cleveland, Ohio. "Just looking out from my office here at Lake Erie, it's hard to believe—but there's a higher concentration of shipping accidents in the Great Lakes than anywhere else in the world that I know of," he said.

"Greater than the Bermuda Triangle?"

"Yes."

This is no small comparison. Ships as well as aircraft disappear with uncanny regularity in the Bermuda Triangle. The differences between the Great Lakes and the Bermuda Triangle tend to emphasize the unknown dangers of the lakes. Unlike the open seas of the Bermuda Triangle, the Great Lakes are completely enclosed freshwater pools. Across the face of the Great Lakes it is almost impossible to be 50 miles from land. The Bermuda Triangle, about 1.5 million square miles, is 16 times larger than all the lakes combined. Because of the irregular shape of the Great Lakes, pilots—aware of dangers within—ordinarily circumnavigate the lakes, even when overflying might be shorter. It is almost impossible for even the slowest aircraft to be more than 20 minutes from land. Today's airliner can cross Lake Erie through the middle in ten minutes. Faster aircraft can do it in much less than four minutes. Over any point on any of the

14

Great Lakes, it is possible for the pilot of any jet airliner to shut down all his engines and literally glide to land. There are hundreds of ground-based, sea-based and air-based radios constantly monitoring emergency frequencies for any sign of trouble.

Aware of the curious incidents over the Great Lakes, the Federal Aviation Administration several years ago instituted a special "Lake Reporting Service"; pilots on Great Lakes overflights make continuous reports to ground stations. A ten-minute delay in such a report automatically launches search-and-rescue operations. This service has saved many lives that would have been lost to ordinary accidents, but the high incidence of inexplicable disasters has remained unaffected.

The happenings in this region have been thoroughly studied and documented by government scientists who specialize in such investigation. For the most part their findings are open to public scrutiny. Most of the files are kept in Washington, D.C., and Ottawa, Ont. The odd characteristics of these occurrences repeat themselves over and over again in definable terms.

Some of the most prominent of these characteristics are discussed in the chapters which follow.

Chapter Two:

SILENT PASSAGE

At work in the Great Lakes is a force that destroys those who venture there with devastating speed and power —a speed and power yet unexplained.

The Aero Commander 560E is a twin-engine corporate-size aircraft. Henry S. Morgan, Shoreham Building, Washington, D.C., once owned one. It was registered N3823C.[1] Based in Atlanta, Ga., it was chartered to business executives who had temporary need for the sleek roomy airplane. On February 12, 1964, N3823C left Atlanta with 40-year-old professional pilot James M. Mixon at the controls. It deadheaded (flew without cargo or passengers) to Danbury, Conn., where it picked up the man who had hired it, George Drake of Wilton, Conn. Drake was a real-estate developer who was considering building stores for S. S. Kresge Co. near Akron, Ohio. For the next two days N3823C made several short flights around Lake Erie shuttling those who were interested in dealing with Drake.

At 8:20 A.M. on February 15, 1964, N3823C left Detroit, Mich. It carried pilot Mixon, Drake and Harry E. Black and Edward Black of Grosse Point Wood, Mich., and at least 4½ hours' fuel. Since it was slightly hazy, Mixon, wary of a possible collision in the heavy traffic around Detroit, asked for radar monitoring until he got into the bright clear sky above the haze. Once in clear air above Lake Erie, N3823C leveled off and accelerated to cruising speeds. The planned destination was only an hour away. All was normal. Weather was excellent. The intended course, however, was over a portion of western Lake Erie long feared for the mysterious things that hap-

16

pen to those who venture there. The intended destination was Akron-Canton (Ohio) Airport.

The *actual* destination was, presumably, Lake Erie.

There is a reasonable doubt, though. The Civil Aeronautics Board's "Factual Report of Investigation," which is open to public inspection, reads as follows:

> A search was organized and conducted under the supervision of the Eastern Air Rescue Center, Robins Air Force Base, Georgia. Units of the Michigan and Ohio Civil Air Patrol and the Royal Canadian Air Force participated in the search. A total of more than 102 hours was flown by 28 aircraft before the search was suspended on February 23, 1964. No location of the aircraft or occupants resulted from this search.

Only one scrap of evidence was ever found. It proved of little value as a clue. It was as mysterious as the lonely logbook of Northwest Flight 2501, which was found floating on Lake Michigan where a DC-4 should have been. It was George Drake's wallet, found 50 miles east of Mixon's intended course. "No other evidence of the aircraft or occupants is known to have been found," explains the report.

The official cause is "undetermined."

Unofficially, the cause is only slightly more specific. The chief investigator prepared a private report, classified confidential to this day. Its conclusions are as follows:

> From the information available, pilot Maxon was capable and qualified for the intended flight. The aircraft N3823C was in apparent good working order. At this time, from the information available, there is no known clue as to what may have occurred on this flight to cause it to crash into Lake Erie.
>
> Though it is impossible to pinpoint the probable cause, *it is the belief of this writer the occurrence that took place must have been very quick, or of a catastrophic nature, or both.* No calls of distress were known to have been made. [Italics mine.]

Harold A. Jacobs, the man who wrote that confidential report, ventured no guess as to what the "quick" and/or "catastrophic" event might have been.

What could happen to an airplane the size of an Aero Commander 560E—or for that matter to a DC-4 like Northwest Flight 2501—flying at enroute altitudes with constant open communication? Certainly the Civil Aeronautics Board ruled wisely when, after considerable study, it put N3823C alongside Northwest 2501 in the small category of disasters with "undetermined" cause.

Pilot T. G. Stevens took off on February 12, 1963, in Canadian civil aircraft number CF-LVJ[2] with passengers J. B. Barclay, R. S. Dutko and J. F. Dowling, all of Niagara Falls, N.Y. The four apparently intended to view from the air the falls which join Lake Erie and Lake Ontario. A number of witnesses on the ground watched as their plane cruised above the river in that direction. The witnesses gave investigators detailed reports on how CF-LVJ began to break up.

Stevens, Barclay, Dutko and Dowling died.

In addition to the reports from ground witnesses, investigators had all the pieces of CF-LVJ and the remains of its occupants with which to work. In such cases it is a simple matter for these experts to determine whether a given component failed before impact or on impact.

CF-LVJ was clearly a case of "inflight structural failure." Specifically, the left wing was snapped off.

Distinguishing between a fatigue fracture and a stress fracture is easy. Fatigue fracturing is a slow process that is supposed to be caught during periodic inspections. The fracture point characteristically shows oxidation that has developed over the life of the fracture. A stress fracture, on the other hand, shows shiny clean metal. It is caused by an extreme force, stronger than the airframe itself. For instance, flying at high speed into the face of a cliff will cause serious stress fractures. But airframes are stronger than most people realize. The wing of CF-LVJ could easily withstand acceleration forces that would render unconscious all the occupants of the airplane. From the way CF-LVJ's wing had been torn off it looked as though the craft had flown through a tornado.

But there was no tornado.

There wasn't even a storm.

In fact, it was a calm day. Surface wind velocity measured at an airport seven miles away was only three miles per hour.

To explain this impossible occurrence, the accident investigators called on government meteorologists. The atmospheric experts conducted a number of tests, including flying highly instrumented airplanes through the same area and dropping smoke bombs and taking dozens of photographs. The results of all this testing were exactly what the meteorologists would have expected had it never been for CF-LVJ. "Attempts to relate the results to actual values of sufficient magnitude to cause the failure of the aircraft wing structure were not successful," wrote the authorities.

The conclusion was clear. Something invisible to ground observers and unknown to engineers and meteorologists must have influenced the course of events. What the force was, no one knows. What is known is that it acted with devastating speed and with strength beyond any known natural phenomena that possibly could prevail undetected.

The *Bannockburn*[3] was a sturdy, steel, British-built ship. She was carrying grain from Port Arthur, Ont., on Lake Superior to Midland, Ont., in Georgian Bay of Lake Huron on November 21, 1902. Capt. James McMaugh of the *Algonquin* was upbound on roughly the opposite course. The *Bannockburn* must have been a majestic sight on this fine day, because Captain McMaugh told his mate to take a look at her. McMaugh's remark caused some confusion in the *Algonquin* pilot house.

The *Bannockburn* was no longer there.

McMaugh was the only one who saw her. He may have felt silly pointing to a blank horizon. The mate may have reserved some doubts about McMaugh. But no one suspected the *Bannockburn* of sinking. McMaugh saw no signs of distress, and a ship cannot sink in the time it takes to look through a pilot-house window. McMaugh was confused by what he saw—or what he thought he saw. He was not sure what had happened. But whatever it was it must have been something more plausible than the *Bannockburn* sinking. That was not even suggested, at least not until several days later. But *something* happened to the *Bannockburn*. She never made it to the eastern end of Lake Superior. Superstitious sailors over the years have reported sighting the *Bannockburn* many times. (See *Rouse Simmons*, Chapter Five, for similar post-disappearance sightings.) But no such sightings have been confirmed, and it is unreasonable to suggest that she is still afloat on Lake Superior 75 years after McMaugh last saw her.

No bodies or wreckage—not a scrap of evidence— have been found. There is no hint as to what became of the *Bannockburn*. No one knows where she is.

The quality of an air traffic controller's life is directly proportional to the quality of weather in his area of responsibility. When weather is bad, all flights must file instrument flight plans in accordance with Instrument Flight Rules. Pilots must follow, and Air Traffic Control must provide, instructions or "clearances" to keep all Instrument Flight Rules flights separated. The combined pressures of safety and efficiency, under the worst conditions, can push men like those who run Milwaukee Approach Control to the limits of human stress.

Fortunately, weather is not that bad most of the time. And on beautiful days like July 21, 1972, controllers barely have a job at all. On such days, the vast majority of aircraft did not even contact approach controllers, since the controllers only handle outlying airspace more than five miles from the airport. When pilots did talk to Approach Control, it was little more than a formality.

That was the situation when conscientious Anderson Duggar, Jr., of Bloomfield Hills, Mich., contacted Milwaukee Approach Control just after 9:00 A.M. on that date. Duggar had left Detroit earlier that morning in his well-equipped and fully fueled multi-engine Piper PA-31. Duggar was an experienced and highly certified pilot with personal business in Milwaukee. To Milwaukee Approach, Duggar was N212AD.[4] The controllers would say that as "Piper November Two One Two Alpha Delta," or simply "Alpha Delta," for short. Presumably Duggar had made a special request for the registration number; his initials were Alpha Delta.

Duggar asked the controller at Milwaukee Approach for radar traffic advisories. He wanted to know if there were other aircraft ahead of him. Duggar's call to Milwaukee Approach was not required, but it was perfectly normal. If Milwaukee Approach could give him radar vectors or directions directly to the airport, it would save Duggar a few minutes. Being advised of interfering traffic also gave Duggar additional safety.

The controller had no problem identifying N212AD's target on his radar display. The target was still flying at enroute altitude 15 miles east of Milwaukee General Mitchell Field. It was over Lake Michigan, about two or three minutes from shore.

It takes about six seconds for a radar antenna like the one in use at General Mitchell Field to sweep a full circle around the sky. At about 9:10 A.M., the radar antenna passed through due east. Simultaneously the approach controller's display painted a bright-green reply from N212AD. The radio was silent, but communication with the target was open. All was normal. About six seconds later as the antenna swept through due east again, N212AD's avionics or radio equipment did not make the usual automatic reply to radar interrogation. The controller turned a knob. There was no primary radar return from N212AD. The controller keyed his transmitter, and asked for a response. There was no answer.

There was no N212AD.

There was no Duggar.

"A search has been conducted but no trace of the airplane or pilot has been found," reads the accident report. "Probable Cause: Miscellaneous, undetermined" was the final verdict.

What happened to N212AD is absolutely incredible to anyone who understands the significance of Duggar's enroute altitude. N212AD was thousands of feet above the surface of Lake Michigan. Had Duggar wanted to put his radio under his arm and jump out of N212AD with no parachute, he still would have had more than 30 seconds to discuss the situation with the approach controller. If an airplane in the clouds suddenly flies into the side of a mountain or comes crashing in short of a runway, no one wonders about the absence of a distress call. There is no time to use the radio in those situations. But as with so many Great Lakes accidents, N212AD fell into another category.

Even though the controllers were able to dispatch rescue craft immediately to the exact spot where N212AD vanished, no trace of Duggar or his aircraft was ever found.

One of the strangest such instant losses at high altitude occurred on May 15, 1956. A Canadian twin-jet CF-100, number 18367,[5] was conducting night-intercept exercises at 33,000 feet (6.25 miles up) while talking to radar control. The interceptor was just northeast of Lake Ontario, when the controller noted that the aircraft was gone. Only seconds had passed since the pilot's last transmission. The transmission had been routine. It was subsequently learned that the jet crashed intact into a convent. The Canadian Air Force could not and has not explained how the pilot got from 33,000 feet to the surface without comment to the controller.

The crash that destroyed N20M[6] was watched by several ground witnesses. They saw how quickly it happened, and consequently there was no mystery about the absence of any distress call. N20M was a Lear Jet 23. It left Detroit Metro Airport on December 15, 1972. Its destination was Lexington, Ky. Its purpose was to pick up cargo. Only the two pilots were aboard. In command was Daniel K. Green, an experienced airline transport pilot. The copilot was an equally experienced airline transport pilot, Harold R. Carroll.

Several witnesses near Detroit watched the sleek jet suddenly pitch forward and dive headlong toward the earth, where it crashed into a gasoline storage tank, killing both pilots and a workman on top of the tank.

The subsequent investigation was one of the most extensive, lasting six months. The still-secret reports associated with the investigation show that every system of the airplane was examined. The brief flight was reconstructed to the smallest detail.

There was no evidence to indicate either mechanical failure or pilot error. It is, nevertheless, a matter of public record that the crash, as described, did happen. It is also a matter of public record that the cause of the crash remains "undetermined." It is doubtful that anyone ever will learn what happened to N20M. But whatever it was, witnesses were unanimous on one point: It happened quickly.

On March 26, 1961, an experienced, 27-year-old commercial pilot was just west of Lake Michigan in Wisconsin, at the controls of a Wittman Tailwind, registration number N11Q.[7] The government's synopsis of the report reads, in part, as follows:

> Just before the crash, about 1720 (5:20 P.M.), the aircraft engine sound was heard to increase in volume. The plane was seen in a steep rolling, high speed descent in which it crashed.
>
> A meticulous and thorough investigation of the accident showed the aircraft had sustained structural failure before ground impact. Failure was induced by negative forces on the horizontal tail surfaces. Calculations showed that the forces were well in excess of the design strength limits of the structure. The airspeed indicator was impact marked at 255 m.p.h.

Unlike the other accidents mentioned in this chapter, this one was assigned a probable cause by the Civil Aeronautics Board. It was "inflight structural failure caused by a high speed maneuver during which forces exceeded the structural ultimate load factor." In other words, the pilot put the airplane into a dive in which he accelerated to such speeds that the airplane was torn apart.

Under the circumstances this probable cause is perfectly plausible, but, unfortunately, it raises more questions than it answers.

Why would an experienced commercial pilot subject an airframe to such incredible stress? Given the board's evidence that the airplane was sound until it began to tear apart, it is not possible for this "accident" to have been truly an accident. Diving an airplane toward the earth at full thrust is not the sort of thing that is done inadvertently. It cannot possibly be done through oversight or carelessness. There was a passenger aboard N11Q. He was almost a stranger to the pilot. Suicide was not indicated. The Civil Aeronautics Board made no suggestion as to whether it was the pilot or some other force that put N11Q in that fatal dive.

In 1892 the *W. H. Gilcher*[8] was the pride of the Great Lakes. One of the first of the huge steel ships, she had immediately set the Great Lakes grain-carrying record. Among other notable records on the *W. H. Gilcher* was the "simple matter of record that the *W. H. Gilcher* on the night of October 28, 1892, vanished from the face of Lake Michigan" (Boyer). As with the other disasters in this chapter, the *W. H. Gilcher* did not slowly fade away. To this day no one knows where or how it disappeared, but it disappeared with frightening speed.

Historians know about the speed because of a single clue recovered the next year. It was the only scrap of evidence ever found. A Captain Stuffelbaum of the steam barge *Hattie B. Perene* found the "stringbacks" that supported the canvas covers on the *Gilcher's* lifeboats. In any ordinary emergency the canvas covers would have been folded back and the lifeboats launched. But the *W. H. Gilcher's* stringbacks bore clear evidence that one of the victims, too terrified to launch the boat in the normal way, had attacked the canvas covers with an ax. He apparently knocked the stringbacks clear, but even in his insane rush he lacked the time to free the lifeboat from its doomed ship. No lifeboats were found. The stringbacks were all that was left to show the terror that prevailed a moment before the *W. H. Gilcher* and her crew vanished forever.

On November 28, 1952, the Beech 35, like the Canadian civil aircraft registered CF-FUV,[9] was a relatively new aircraft. On that day CF-FUV was on the last leg of a flight from Edmonton to Toronto. It had departed Houghton, Mich., and proceeded eastbound along the southern

24

shore of Lake Superior. United States radar stations, constantly scanning the border, kept close contact with CF-FUV. If pilot F. Jake experienced a problem, he had only to extend his arm to the radio microphone, key the transmitter and say "Uniform Victor, Mayday." If he had done it slowly, it would have taken four seconds. The radar controllers already had his position. Dispatching rescue craft to the spot would be easy. F. Jake did experience a problem. But he never transmitted his distress.

About 40 miles northwest of Grand Marias, Mich., and 35 miles northeast of Marquette, Mich., CF-FUV, F. Jake and his three passengers flew away. They vanished silently from the radar screen. The position was noted by the radar controller. But "despite an extensive search no trace of the aircraft or occupants was found," says the Canada Department of Transport summary accident report. The scientists who studied this strange case concluded that "for undetermined reasons CF-FUV disappeared in Lake Superior."

Though CF-FUV preceded the *Edmund Fitzgerald* (see Chapter One) by several years, they vanished in nearby locations. Dozens of other ships and aircraft have vanished for no apparent reason near this point in Lake Superior (see Chapter Fifteen).

After discharging his cargo of coal at Sarnia, Ont., on the southern tip of Lake Huron, Capt. Fred Sharpsteen set sail on the schooner *Hunter Savidge*[10] and headed her north-northwest toward Alpena, Mich. It was August 20, 1899. The winds were light until about 4:00 P.M., just off Point aux Barques. Then the schooner found herself becalmed beneath the hot August sun. Becalmed, that is, until a strange wind came up. A wind that, with no warning, drove the bow of the ship beneath the surface, exploded the sails "like cannon shot" (Boyer), snapped the shrouds, lines and chains, completely rolled the ship over, and left her right side up but almost completely submerged. It was a horrifying ten seconds for the crew and passengers, five of whom were lost. Ten seconds was all the wind lasted. The *Hunter Savidge* was becalmed again, as quickly as she had been attacked. The ship was a total wreck, her survivors clinging to the almost worth-less hulk. They were rescued by the steamer *McVittie*. There were several witnesses on board the *McVittie*. They saw the ten-second attack on the *Hunter Savidge* and substantiated the report of the *Hunter Savidge* survivors.

But witnesses and survivors notwithstanding, no one has explained exactly was it was that tore the *Hunter Savidge* to pieces.

The wreck, still afloat, disappeared a short time after the survivors were taken aboard the *McVittie*.

On June 18, 1872, the schooner *Jamaica*,[11] 318 tons, was making her way through Lake Huron with a cargo of 18,000 bushels of wheat from Chicago to Oswego, N.Y., at the eastern end of Lake Ontario. As described by historians of the time (Mansfield), she was hit by a strange "whirlwind." The ship under command of David Bothwell was

> immediately capsized. The crew clug to the vessel until a small boat from the schooner *Starlight* went to their rescue. The *Starlight* had met the same kind of accident a year or two before this at the same place.

After the city of Greenville, Mich., bought a Bell 47J helicopter from the Canadian Ministry of Transport in Ottawa, Ont., the helicopter was given a United States registration number. Canadian aircraft registration numbers all begin with "CF." United States aircraft numbers begin with "N." This helicopter's new number was N37755.[12] On April 19, 1974, an experienced commercial pilot picked up N37755 to deliver the well-maintained helicopter to Greenville. Weather was perfect. Above was a beautiful clear blue sky. Several ground witnesses later recalled seeing the helicopter proceeding on course with no sign of trouble. But as it neared the northeast shore of Lake Ontario,

> the helicopter was observed to be cruising between 700 feet to 900 feet AGL [above ground level] when it yawed left then right. The nose pitched up then down. The helicopter then inverted and sections became detached as it plummeted to the ground. The main body

burst into flames on ground impact and intense fire followed.

Subsequent examination of the wreckage showed that the alert pilot, realizing his predicament, had begun emergency procedures in preparation for the crash.

The battery and generator switches were found in the off position. The magneto switch was in the off position. The mixture control was in the lean position [this cut off fuel to the engine].

The pilot's rational behavior under such violent battering is truly incredible. Unfortunately, however, the proficient pilot's efforts to minimize the impending disaster were of no consequence. Something was rolling and tumbling the helicopter so violently that N37755 and its pilot were doomed to instant destruction.

Transport Canada Air's thorough investigation concluded that "the available evidence indicates that the pilot was faced with an inflight emergency of an undetermined nature." Despite their meticulous examination of each piece of wreckage, there simply was no evidence of either pilot error or mechanical failure. Whatever the "inflight emergency" was, it occurred quickly with no clues left behind.

A similar accident a number of years earlier and farther east on the St. Lawrence showed how really elusive an explanation can be. It was October 22, 1959. An experienced Canadian Department of Transport pilot, R. F. Lavack, was at the controls of another Bell 47J. Owned and operated by the government, it was registered as CF-GXZ.[13] It was skimming 100 feet over the water when Lavack

experienced a severe vibration and partial loss of control. An autorotation landing [on a convenient island] was executed immediately. The aircraft cut a swath through second growth spruce trees in its descent sustaining damage only to the tail rotor and tail rotor drive shaft.

Lavack and his passenger walked away unharmed to describe later exactly what had happened. Investigators

27

could never explain how this accident was possible. The helicopter, upon their examination, was in almost perfect condition. The only thing damaged was the tail rotor. After it was repaired, the helicopter was flown away with no hint of a vibration. Since the original problem therefore had to be in the tail rotor, the damaged components were meticulously studied. But the results of that examination showed that the only damage was sustained on impact. This left the investigators with a problem. They had a helicopter—subsequently proved to be in perfect condition—and an experienced professional pilot who claimed that he had been forced to land the helicopter to save himself. Their conclusion was "vibration of undetermined extent and origin caused the pilot to attempt an emergency autorotation landing in unsuitable territory resulting in damage to the tail rotor and its drive shaft."

Dr. Joseph Allen Hynek has associated such vibrations with UFO phenomena. (Unlike most "scientists" studying UFO phenomena, Dr. Hynek is generally regarded as a serious student of astronomy. He has been director of the Lindheimer Astronomical Research Center at Northwestern University, where he still teaches, and chairman of the Department of Astronomy. He had served as Associate Director of the Smithsonian Astrophysical Observatory in Cambridge, Mass., and was once head of its NASA-sponsored satellite tracking program. Hynek also was consultant to the U.S. Air Force Project Blue Book, which was the government's most concerted effort to find answers to UFO questions. He is currently the scientific director of the Center for the UFO Studies.) He describes one such case, on April 14, 1957, when two women watched a UFO land less than 300 feet away. It was described as

a curious metallic machine in the form of a big top about five feet tall. Just as it landed, a deafening rattle was heard coming from a metallic road sign some 15 to 20 feet from the landing site. The sign had been set into violent vibration.

The cries of the women and the noise from the sign were heard by a man nearly 1000 feet away. Thinking that there had been an accident, he went rushing down to them. He arrived in time to see the "top" jump off the road to a height of about 20 feet, turn, and land a second time, this time on another road, which forked from the first.

As it turned, it flew over a second road sign, and this one likewise vibrated violently, resonating as though it had been subjected to "violent shocks repeated at a rapid cadence." The machine however made no sound itself.[14]

Incidentally, when local authorities later placed a compass next to the vibrated sign the compass deviated 15 degrees. Next to other signs the deviation was only four degrees.

Sunday, October 10, 1971, was a perfect flying day. John W. Chadwick and Leonard Grainger decided to go from Salem, Mich., to Owosso, Mich., between Lake Huron and Lake Michigan. Grainger took off first in the slower Cessna 172. Grainger's wife waited to go with Chadwick in the faster PA-24, registration number N9015P.[15]

As prearranged between the two pilots, radio communication was established on frequency 122.9 MHz. Chadwick in N9015P radioed to the Cessna, "I'm passing you on the right."

Grainger and a passenger, who was also a pilot, looked to their right and ahead. There was N9015P pulling away from them at its faster cruising speed of about 150 miles per hour. N9015P was in perfectly level flight. There was no unusual turbulence. Grainger watched the PA-24 Comanche with his wife Hazel aboard—as it began to disintegrate. The other pilot with Grainger gave this description:

Mr. Grainger and I saw the rudder and vertical fin flopping right then left and then it came off going to the right. The tail then came up and the plane went into a 10 degree right bank. A few seconds later the left part of the stabalator came off. The plane then went into a right spiral made about five turns and crashed.

Everyone aboard the PA-24 was killed.

Subsequent examination disclosed the exact sequence of destruction within the empennage of the PA-24. But no one has determined why it occurred.

Weather was cloudy three or four miles south of Georgian Bay and visibility was restricted to two miles on September 26, 1970, when a sleek Cessna 210-5, Canadian registration CF-OUR,[16] was ripped apart in midair. Examination of the wreckage revealed the same kind of stress fractures that marked the extraordinary demolition of CF-LVJ on February 12, 1963, discussed earlier in this chapter. This time it was the right, instead of the left, wing that was ripped apart like aluminum foil. CF-OUR struck the ground at high speed and burned. Four were killed.

Anthony R. Farinacci, pilot of N2347U[17] on December 19, 1966, made it plainly clear that he was aware of his predicament. The weather was good—4500-foot ceiling and seven miles' visibility—when Farinacci left Erie, Pa., on the south shore of Lake Erie. Farinacci, unlike the other pilots discussed in this chapter, was not highly experienced. He became lost after leaving Erie. After an hour he called Erie Tower for help. Cleveland Air Route Traffic Control Center (Cleveland Center), working through Erie Tower, was able to make radar contact with N2347U. Through Erie Tower, Cleveland Center gave N2347U directions that would take him back to Erie. Six minutes later the following series of desperate, shrill screams were transmitted over the Erie Tower frequency by N2347U:

I'm upside down or something—I can't ah . . .
I'm not spinning now—but I'm . . .
I'm not spinning but . . .
I can't seem (unintelligible). I can't seem to get my (unintelligible).
I'm losing altitude awful fast now and I can't seem to get my horizon straight.

The transmissions ended abruptly.
N2347U's radar target simultaneously disappeared from

Cleveland Center radar a short distance from shore over Lake Erie. Search and rescue efforts were launched immediately. Search craft were directed by Cleveland Center to the precise location of the disappearance.

No trace of N2347U has ever been found.

All that is known is that whatever happened to N2347U happened quickly.

A Cessna 195B, registration number N4450C,[18] made it all the way across Lake Erie from Ontario to Sandusky, Ohio, with its pilot and two passengers on September 9, 1963. Weather was nice. N4450C, close to its destination, was ripped apart in midair. It plummeted to the ground and hit the concrete embankment of the Sandusky yacht basin. All aboard were killed.

A Beech 35, United States registration N2752V,[19] was speeding almost due west from Kapuskasing, Ont., to Kenora, Ont., with C. P. Day at the controls on June 8, 1955. As it passed north of Lake Superior, N2752V made a position report and estimated his next checkpoint at about 3:00 P.M.

On June 14, 1955, searchers finally found the tardy aircraft. The remains of the two aboard were mangled badly. A close examination of the wreckage was made, and the conclusion of that examination was "the wings and empennage (tail section) separated from the aircraft during flight for reasons that were not conclusively determined and it crashed to the ground inverted."

There is little doubt that the pilot of the twin jet CF-101 Canadian Air Force interceptor, number 18112,[20] knew he was in trouble on August 23, 1954. He was near Ajax, Ont., on the north shore of Lake Ontario. He bailed out. He explained later that the aircraft became impossible to control. Publicly, the Canadian Defense Headquarters refuses to reveal the cause of the accident. The official cause is classified secret. I have seen this secret file. It says the scientists who studied the case *could not determine* what caused the jet to become unmanageable.

To say that these experts of accident investigation cannot determine what caused an accident is amazing to those familiar with the state of the art. These detectives rarely fail in their efforts to reconstruct a disaster—rarely, that is, except in the Great Lakes. A good example is the last flight of N1539D.[21] Pilot and sole occupant Willard F. Bierema was flying over the west end of Lake Erie from Alliance, Ohio, to Detroit, Mich., on July 20, 1962. This is an area of Lake Erie long feared for the strange things that have happened to those who ventured there. On July 20, 1962, sometime between 4:00 and 5:00 P.M., the aircraft was ripped apart in midair for no apparent reason. The accident file is only a brief summary of the investigation into the disaster. In this respect it is like all accident files. The following excerpt is quoted, not because the reader should fully understand it, but rather because it serves to illustrate the incredible perspicacity of the scientists who specialize in deciphering tragedy:

A comprehensive study was made of the wreckage and detailed plots were drawn showing its ground distribution. A reasonable description of the sequence of the aircraft's breakup became possible after examination of failures in the structure, observation of modes of these failures, consideration of weather data and probable trajectories of wreckage items. Trajectory studies indicate the aircraft was flying at about 2000 feet above ground at the time of the breakup at a relative high speed and possibly in a shallow dive.

The first failures which occurred are considered to have been the almost simultaneous downward collapse of the leading edge of both wing panels and a downward displacement of the rear fuselage. The result of these failures was a violent nose down pitching with loss of the empennage [tail section] assemblies and the right outer wing. It is possible that spar capstrip failures occurred at the time of the leading edge displacement. Indications are that the vertical fin was the first component to become detached from the aircraft. The right elevator was thrown relatively intact but portions of the left elevator were not found and some premature failure in the latter component could have occurred prior to loss of the fin. The left wing became detached in an upward direction at considerably lower altitude. The fuselage apparently struck the ground at an angle of approximately 70 degrees while travelling in a direction between 128 degrees and 168 degrees [southeast].

There appears to have been a swing to the right [in the flight path] at the time of the first failure, followed by a spiral dive or spin to the left.

No major fault in the airframe, engine or controls was found which would have caused difficulty in flight. Some previous repair work to the airframe was of poor quality, but did not in itself lead to the aircraft breakup. The breakup came as a result of aerodynamic forces beyond the design strength of the structure. There is considerable evidence to indicate that these aerodynamic forces were the result of local weather conditions.

Subsequent to the analysis, the "probable cause" seemed almost comical—or at least as comical as a man's death can be. It said that "parts of the aircraft failed through overstressing."

Air Force jet pilot John William Wilson of Cincinnati stated positively that he knew something was wrong with his F-86 Thursday afternoon, August 27, 1953, over southern Lake Michigan. The pilot of an F-86 does not have to pick up a microphone and raise it to his lips in order to transmit a message. The microphone is already strapped in place and he can key his transmitter by pressing a button on the control stick. Wilson did just that. He made a fragmentary distress call from 15,000 feet. He was cut off in midsentence. Search crews found no trace of the plane or pilot, despite the fact that Lt. Gill Garrett, in another F-86, witnessed the tragedy.

"I was trailing by about 500 feet," he said. "I heard Wilson call base saying there was an emergency and indicating he would bail out. But almost as he spoke the plane flew apart. No parachute was seen and I believe Wilson never got out of his seat," Garrett said.[22]

At work in the Great Lakes is a force that destroys those who venture there with devastating speed and power —a speed and power yet unexplained.

Chapter Three:

TWINKLING HARM

Strange objects capable of silent yet incredibly power-
ful acceleration, maneuvering high above the Great Lakes,
have been watched by competent observers. They operate
as if guided by an intelligence, resemble no publicly known
aircraft and remain unidentified.

At 1:00 A.M. on a summer night in 1950 two White
Fish Bay, Wisc., policemen were disturbed by what they
saw hovering in the sky above Lake Michigan. White
Fish Bay is a suburb of Milwaukee. The men noted the
object several miles out over the lake east-southeast
of their position. They watched the eerie red object glow-
ing for ten minutes. Then it disappeared. They were
awed. They had worked nights for a long time. They
had never seen anything like it before. After it disappeared
they rushed to report it to the United States Coast Guard.
The Coast Guard Milwaukee Station dispatched a Coast
Guard cutter. The crew of the cutter never saw the object.
They did find something unusual. It was a United States
Naval Research vessel working in Lake Michigan at 2:00
A.M.[1]

The Coast Guard captain asked the captain of the
naval vessel what his ship was doing in Lake Michigan.

The naval officer said, "Maneuvers."

The Coast Guard captain asked if anyone on board
the research ship had seen the strange object that shore
authorities had reported.

The naval officer said, "No."

The question of what the glimmering red light over
Lake Michigan was has never been resolved.

The Coast Guard lacked time to investigate further.

Within three hours it was to launch the biggest search in the history of Lake Michigan. It was the morning of June 24, 1950.

It was the morning the Coast Guard was notified that Northwest Airlines Flight 2501 (see Chapter One) had vanished somewhere east-southeast of Milwaukee.

February 6, 1961, was an exciting night all across the northeastern United States for hundreds of skywatchers. Government authorities were deluged by citizens wanting some kind of explanation for the blinking objects that they had seen. Neither the North American Air Defense Command nor the Smithsonian Astrophysical Observatory in Cambridge, Mass., was able to explain the phenomena.

But another event that night subsequently proved even more baffling to Civil Aeronautics Board investigators.[2]

Peter Dekeita, 29, was a highly qualified airline co-pilot. He had been flying Viscounts for five years. He was considered "well qualified in" the PA-22. At about 3:00 P.M. Dekeita and his passengers, on a pleasure flight, returned safely to Howell Airport, Blue Island, Ill. It was the aircraft's homebase. They all left the airport together. At 4:00 P.M. Dekeita returned to the airport alone. He departed Howell Airport in N9402D[3] just before 5:30 P.M. A few minutes later he talked to Joliet Flight Service Station. He was directly over Merrill C. Meigs Field, opposite downtown Chicago on the shore of Lake Michigan. "Visibility unlimited with scattered cirrus," he told Joliet Radio. That was excellent weather—a perfect evening for flying on the shore of Lake Michigan. Two minutes later Dekeita—a calm professional with more than 5000 hours of piloting experience—began transmitting in a garbled and shaky-pitched voice (according to the men at Joliet Radio).

"Having trouble, going into lake," Dekeita screamed.

They asked for his position. His only reply was, "Having trouble, going into lake."

The shore ice on Lake Michigan extended some 15 miles eastward. The following morning, N9402D, Dekeita's mangled body still at the controls, was found nosedown on the lake ice about four miles from Meigs

Field. There had been no fire. The wreckage was intact. This incident has subsequently proved one of the strangest tragedies in the history of civil aviation.

Investigation revealed that the aircraft struck the ice while in a nosedown attitude. Speed at impact was well above that for a normal landing and the engine was developing substantial power at impact. There was no indication of engine failure or malfunction. Inspection revealed that all controls were intact and were capable of normal operation at impact.

This was mystery enough. How could an experienced airline pilot, flying in beautifully clear weather, crash a perfectly functioning airplane four miles from a well-lighted airport? For that matter, what was Dekeita doing four miles from the airport, well outside the normal approach distance for his aircraft? Though several have tried to answer these questions, all have admitted failure.

What happened to Dekeita and N9402D is simply not plausible.

But there was a mysterious addition to this accident report: "Examination of the stabilizer adjustment yoke, which is controlled from the cockpit, placed the horizontal stabilizer trim in the full nosedown position." Trim is a kind of control's control. The pilot moves the elevator (the horizontal flap on the tail of the airplane) in order to point the airplane up or down. He adjusts the elevator trim to relieve pressure on the control wheel so that he does not have to hold constant pressure against the wheel.

Why would Dekeita have the airplane trimmed nosedown all the way?

Like all the other questions about this crash, that question too likely will remain unanswered.

Full nosedown trim is hardly used. The full nosedown limit is only approached in a sustained high-speed, high-power-setting, rapid descent. It might also be approached in an area of exceptionally strong updrafts if the pilot wanted to get maximum speed while maintaining level flight, but no such meteorological condition existed that night.

All that is known is that Dekeita trimmed the airplane

36

for a rapid shallow descent and went screaming down into the lake ice with the throttle wide open.

Could it have been suicide? It is highly unlikely for a number of reasons. Dekeita was screaming his distress over the radio just before he crashed into the lake ice. Dekeita's death dive could have been averted right up to the last second. Consequently his screams are hardly consistent with suicide. Besides, an experienced pilot intent on self-destruction would use some other maneuver that would bring the airplane to the ground either vertical or inverted. Beyond these simple facts, the accident investigators looked into Dekeita's background and ruled out suicide.

Non-pilots might confuse the importance of the trim, thinking it caused the accident. This could not be the case. The trim on this airplane could easily be overpowered. Besides, the trim could be changed almost as quickly as the wheel could be pulled back. The trim could not cause the accident, but its strange position is almost certainly related to the crash. Presumably whatever it was that destroyed N9402D did so in a way that caused the terrified pilot to trim the airplane full nosedown.

What could cause that?

Nothing the Civil Aeronautics Board investigators could imagine.

Nothing I can imagine.

The Chicago Tribune reported the next day that it had received many calls from readers who had seen strange colored lights flashing in the sky. The newspaper said the night lights must have been flares sent up by rescue craft. That explanation failed to explain the fact that these blinking lights were seen all across the rest of the northeastern United States. Could these lights have been UFOs? And could these UFOs have sent N9402D to its doom?

UFO expert Dr. Joseph Allen Hynek says that light-in-the-night-sky reports often fail to qualify as genuine UFOs because:

An experienced investigator readily recognizes most of these for what they are: bright meteors, aircraft landing lights, balloons, planets, violent twinkling stars, searchlights, advertising lights on planes, refueling missions, etc.[4]

I have seen and quickly identified not only "bright meteors, aircraft landing lights, balloons, planets," etc., but water reflections, cloud reflections and afterimages as well. I have never seen any nocturnal lights that caused me the least puzzlement. But many pilots, more experienced than I, frequently report being tracked over the Great Lakes by nocturnal lights which they cannot identify.

Enroute traffic on instrument flight plans is ordinarily controlled by a handful of "centers" scattered across the continent. The events discussed so far in this chapter all fell within the airspace controlled by Chicago Center. I spent several hours talking with the air traffic controllers who work nights at Chicago Center. Most readily and openly admitted that they frequently get reports from experienced pilots who see unidentified objects at high altitudes. Their superiors were equally open in confirming the situation.

It was difficult to quantify the frequency of these reports. The average controller worked 50 nights a year covering five of the 60 discrete sectors and reported about three or four such encounters each year. This would be about 70 reports a year, except that some might be duplicates, since a pilot of a high-speed aircraft might talk to two or more controllers in the course of a few minutes.

For no apparent reason, most of the reports originate from westbound traffic at high altitude.

Though the concentration of such reports in the early-morning hours puzzles the controllers, it does not surprise me. A pilot is much more likely to make such a report at that time. One reason for this is that the radio frequencies are less congested, leaving more time for conversation that does not directly involve air traffic

38

control. Another reason is that embarrassment would be at a minimum, since fewer pilots would be listening.

Typically the pilot report comes as a question to the controller. The pilot wants to know if traffic control is painting a target, usually stationary within 30 miles. (Stationary, in this case, means the same course and speed as the aircraft.) Though the controllers try, "we never can get radar contact," was the typical conclusion expressed with some frustration.[5] The controller reports the incident to the watch desk, where it is discarded because of no radar contact.

None of the air traffic controllers with whom I talked at Chicago Center could explain the pilot sightings.

Dr. Hynek has documented a report made by a professional astronomer of an incident that occurred in a town in the Great Lakes region, Walkerton, Ont. The man had been notified by a relative (who was a newspaperman) of a "light" that provincial police had been attempting to follow in their cars. According to this trained observer:

We followed country roads until we came within 100 yards of the object. It was hovering around a large tree, which stood alone in the center of a cultivated field. The tree was about 100 yards distant and about 120 feet high. The object, which subtended an angle of about ¼ degrees (giving it a physical diameter of less than three feet), appeared circular in shape and was thus probably a spheroid. It was highly luminous against the dark sky background and changed color through the whole visible spectral range with a period of ∼ 2 seconds (rather irregular period). Because it was rather bright, I may have slightly overestimated the angular size, and ¼ degrees should perhaps be considered an upper limit. A lower limit would certainly be ⅛ degrees.

The object appeared to be examining the tree rather closely. It circled the upper branches, ranging from 50 to 100 feet off the ground, passing in front of the tree, then clearly visible through the branches on passing behind the tree again. It continued this apparent "observation" of the tree for several minutes while we watched. Then, anxious for a picture, we climbed the perimeter fence and started slowly toward the tree facing due west. We had not gone more than 10 feet before it "noticed" us and noiselessly accelerated at a very high rate, headed almost directly south, disappearing over the horizon (on a slightly rising trajectory) in about 2½ seconds. (I consider my length of time estimates to be quite reliable as I was actively engaged in track and field at the time and thus quite competent at this type of estimation. Even under such exceptional circumstances these figures are most probably within + or − 20 per cent.)

Several observations about the object:

1. It was certainly too small to contain human life;

2. It had no apparent physical surface features apart from the circular shape it presented—possibly because the "surface" was highly luminous;

3. It moved deliberately and purposefully in its "inspection" of the tree, pausing slightly at apparent "points of interest" and giving the distinct impression of "intelligent" behavior;

4. Its motion was completely silent, even the final acceleration;

5. It was definitely not any natural physical phenomenon I have ever encountered or read about (I'm sure you are familiar with what I refer to—"marsh gas" and the like);

6. It was definitely not a distant astronomical object. It was clearly visible alternately through the branches of the tree and obscuring the branches of the tree, fixing its distance quite exactly;

7. It was definitely seen by competent witnesses (including several police officers) besides myself;

8. On acceleration from the tree it almost certainly should have exceeded the speed of sound. There was no accoustical disturbance whatever. (My uncle attempted to take a picture of it as it accelerated, but the result was not good enough to publish due to our excessive distance from the object, and its rapid motion, which combined to produce a very faint blurred image.)

The salient points to consider are these: the object appeared to be governed by some intelligence, and it did not behave as would a physical phenomenon as we understand it.[6]

One evening last year, citizens of Sudbury, Ont., just

inside the north shore of Lake Huron, began reporting brilliant eerie lights hovering low in the sky, then suddenly shooting straight upward at tremendous speeds.[7] It was 3:00 A.M. local time. Regional Police Inspector Frank Singer said two of his officers sighted four objects, three stationary and one moving in a jerky circular motion. Two other policemen spotted an object so bright that it lit up the clouds in the area. Inspector Singer said, after a look at one object through binoculars, that "it appeared to be cylindrical in shape and traveling in circles. The object was kept in visual contact until 7 A.M."

At the Falconbridge radar station, the commanding officer, Maj. Robert Oliver, said that he and five others at the military base saw three mysterious objects in the sky. Major Oliver described the incident as follows:

> We saw the same things many of the local citizens saw. I got a call from my operations officer about 6 A.M. and we went up the hill, and lo and behold, there were three bright yellow objects.
> We viewed these objects through binoculars and weren't able to make any identification at all.

Falconbridge is a North American Air Defense Command radar station. And Oliver, as certainly as anyone, should have been able to identify the phenomenon.

He could not.

The North American Air Defense Command was painting unidentified radar targets in the area. The U.S. Air Force scrambled two F-106 interceptors from Selfridge Air Force Base at the southern tip of Lake Huron. Minutes later the sophisticated jets were being directed by North American Air Defense Command directly to the radar targets.

The interceptors never made visual contact.

Capt. Gordon Hilchie, spokesman for the North American Air Defense Command, said that when the objects were tracked on radar, they were over the north shore of Lake Huron. One object shot upward from 26,000 feet to 45,000 feet, where it "stopped awhile, then moved up very quickly to 72,000 feet."[8] Lt. Col. Brian Wooding, director of the 22nd North American Air Defense Command Center, described the incident as follows:

> We get quite a few UFO reports but to my knowledge this is about the only one we've actually seen on radar and the only time we've gone to the point of scrambling interceptors.
>
> The jets were scrambled because the indications were there was something very evident to a large number of people, and because we did manage to get some sort of radar sighting.[9]

These UFOs were tracked intermittently on radar for six hours. The timing and location of the incident is of particular interest, although no one at the North American Air Defense Command knew it at the time. The incident occurred on November 11, 1975.

Perhaps the most startling aspect of this unexplainable sighting is that it began less than six hours after the Edmund Fitzgerald *(see Chapter One) unexplainably and instantly vanished from the face of Lake Superior only 100 miles to the west.*

It was near this same spot that in 1975 swallowed the *Fitzgerald* that in 1953 a U.S. Air Force F-86 jet interceptor with two aboard instantly disappeared forever. According to some students of that inconceivable event, the F-86 was destroyed by a UFO it had been sent to intercept. The Air Force will not confirm this. Donald Keyhoe, who studied the incident, describes what he learned:

> No trace was found of the airmen, the jet or the UFO.
>
> The search was still on when Truax AFB gave the Associated Press this official release:
>
> "The plane was followed by radar until it merged with an object 70 miles off Keweenaw Point in Upper Michigan."
>
> In view of AF [Air Force] secrecy this was a surprising admission. The statement appeared in an early edition of the *Chicago Tribune*, headed, "JET, TWO ABOARD, VANISHED OVER LAKE SUPERIOR." Then AF Headquarters killed the story.

Denying the jet had merged with anything, the AF said that radar operators had misread the scope. The reported UFO, it stated, had been an offcourse Canadian airliner which the F-86 had intercepted and identified. After this, the AF speculated, the pilot evidently had been stricken with vertigo and the jet had crashed in the lake.

The Canadian airlines quickly denied any flights in the area. Expert pilots also hit at the AF explanation: Moncla [the F-86 pilot in command] could have switched on the automatic pilot until the vertigo passed; also Wilson [second pilot] could have taken over temporarily.[10]

Perhaps the strongest evidence that UFOs might be directly linked to the destruction of aircraft in this area is what UFO buffs call the Walesville, N.Y., case. Keyhoe describes the case as it began just southeast of Lake Ontario:

The most outstanding case involved an AF interceptor crew. Just before noon, on July 1, 1954, an unknown flying object was tracked over New York State by Griffiss AFB radar. An F-94 Starfire jet was scrambled and the pilot climbed steeply toward the target, guided by his radar observer. When a gleaming disc-shaped machine became visible he started to close in.

Abruptly a furnacelike heat filled both cockpits. Gasping for breath, the pilot jettisoned the canopy. Through a blur of heat waves he saw the radar observer bail out. Stunned, without even thinking, he ejected himself from the plane.

The cool air and the jerk of his opening parachute aroused him. He was horrified to see the jet diving toward the heart of a town.

The F-94, screaming down into Walesville, N.Y., smashed through a building and burst into flames. Plunging on, the fiery wreckage careened into a car. Four died in the holocaust—a man and his wife and their two infant children. Five other Walesville residents were injured, two of them seriously.

Soon after the pilot came down, at the edge of town, a reporter appeared on the scene. Still half dazed, the pilot told him about the strange heat. Before he could

43

tell the whole story, an AF car arrived. The pilot and the radar observer were hurried back to Griffiss AFB. Interviews were prohibited, and when the Walesville reporter's story of the sudden heat was published the AF quickly denied it. There was no mystery, headquarters told the press, merely engine trouble.

Although I investigated this case in 1954, there was one angle I did not learn until early '68. While the AF was rechecking the Walesville disaster, also another heat injury case, a headquarters officer I knew gave me the information:

"That F-94 pilot said there was a separate effect besides the heat. Something made his mind black out—he couldn't even remember bailing out. He did recall the sudden heat and he saw the radar observer eject himself. But everything was a blank from then on until his parachute opened. That partly snapped him out of it, but he still had a peculiar dazed feeling.

"The medicos told him it was the intense heat that caused the blackout. And they said the dazed feeling probably came from seeing the jet crash in Walesville. But he didn't believe them. He was sure there was something else besides the heat."[11]

UFO expert Hynek, along with Jacques Vallee, also studied the same case. They wrote as follows:

There was a picture in *The New York Times* the next day of the town in flames with the main engine of the jet in the town square—four people were killed in the crash.

. . . it was a mechanical malfunction all right, but the malfunction was caused by a UFO. In this case in Rome, N.Y. [Griffiss Air Force Base, 45 miles southeast of Lake Ontario], July 2, 1954, there was a dense cloud cover . . . On the radar they picked up an unknown object. They sent two jets up. One stayed in the clouds all the time. The other one was at a higher altitude looking for the object. The two pilots said that they saw the thing and it was coming close to them and then they described something they called a "heat wave." The temperature rose in the cockpit so that they couldn't operate the airplane anymore. They could hardly read the instruments, so they thought the plane

44

was going to burst into flames. Well, they bailed out and landed safely and are still alive.[12]

Vallee later told me in a personal interview (September 27, 1976) that the pilot was Lt. William E. Atkins, 24, of Dutton, Va., and the radar pilot was Henry Coudon, 26, Perryville, Md. Vallee said the pilot landed near Westmoreland, N.Y., and the radar pilot parachuted down near Cary Corner, N.Y.

Chapter Four:

CALM DAYS LAST FOREVER

Ancient Chippewa superstition describes a giant sturgeon in Lake Superior. The huge legendary fish is capable of swallowing a whole ship. It can, with the flick of a fin, churn into boiling violence a small spot on the surface of the lake. Many Chippewa braves have seen either the fish or clear evidence of it.

The fish has not been seen by a white man who has lived to report it.

Factual origin of the legend is unknown.

The *Leafield*[1] was a 4453-ton freighter owned by the Algoma Central Railway. During the summer of 1913 the *Leafield* was steaming railroad rails across the geographic center of Lake Superior. The surface was perfectly calm. The sky was perfectly clear. Nothing changed around or over the *Leafield*. Something odd did happen to the small spot of water on which the *Leafield* floated.

Without warning and with no indication of wind, the waters began to seethe and heave. Great seas from opposing directions poured over her from starboard and port. Plates and frames straining under the weight of the water that had swept over her, the *Leafield* was seemingly in the very center of a cyclonic gale except that the sun was shining; the skies above were clear blue and there was no wind.

Shortly however, the ship was once again in calm water, and except for twisted railings and battered deck gear there was no evidence that the vessel had been in violent water.

The *Leafield* was repaired quickly and returned to service. That fall she sank somewhere near Angus Island in Lake Superior. All hands were lost. Both the summer accident and the subsequent destruction of the ship are a matter of record.

The summer accident remains unexplained.

Several days after that strange event, the *James E. Davidson*,[2] a 6000-ton grain carrier, was steaming across the same water. The record of what happened speaks for itself:

> While proceeding through a heavy snowstorm the *Davidson* was suddenly confronted by a single, tremendous sea [wave]. It thundered aboard directly over the bow, jarring the ship to its very stern frame. In the firehold men were sent tumbling, dishes cascaded from the galley racks and the captain was catapulted from his bunk. The anchor windlass [winch] was torn from its bedplates and its controls smashed. Both anchors dropped from their pockets while tons of chain writhed madly about in the chain locker, tearing out the hawsepipes and loosening bow plates. Far down by the head and making water steadily, the *Davidson* just made the Soo locks, almost in sinking condition. When drydocked for survey the inspectors found a great dent, ten feet long in the ship's bottom.

The incident has never been fully explained.

The *Hibou*[3] was a small Canadian passenger steamer of 308 tons. In 1936 she was 29 years old. On November 21, 1936, she left her dock in Owen Sound Bay in Georgian Bay of Lake Huron with a small cargo of flour and general merchandise. The purpose of the trip was to test a new compass. The *Hibou* was still in the calm bay only two miles from her dock when, without warning, and for no apparent reason, a single devastating wave destroyed her. The source of this destructive force is still unknown. It came as an unwelcome surprise to most of the crew. They were lounging below deck in their pajamas with no reason to suspect any problem. One deckhand, Scotty Smart, recalled the incident as follows:

We were out testing a new compass. Suddenly as we rounded a point, the engine stopped. Without warning the boat lurched and then overturned. Most of us were in our pajamas, and I think those missing were trapped below decks, except for Capt. [Norman] McKay. He was standing on the side of the boat, sending up flares in hope of attracting rescuers.

Ten were saved. Seven perished. No reason for the disaster has yet been proposed.

Charles Berlitz, in his now famous book *The Bermuda Triangle*, has described strikingly similar incidents in that region of the Atlantic Ocean. One such case was reported by the flight crew of a jet airliner. They had an excellent view of the localized phenomenon. Berlitz' account is as follows:

The unusual sighting, first reported by the copilot, took place at 1:30 P.M., 20 minutes after takeoff, when the jet was at an altitude of 31,000 feet. The copilot suddenly noticed, about five miles to starboard [right] from the route the jet was following, that the ocean was rising to a great round mound as if from an underwater atomic explosion, and that it looked like "a big cauliflower" in the water. He immediately called the captain's and the flight engineer's attention to it and they observed it in detail for about 30 seconds, and then unfastened their seat belts and climbed over to starboard for a still better view. The rolling titanic mound of water attained, in their judgement, a diameter of half a mile to a mile, with a height of perhaps half its width. Understandably, the captain did not go back for a closer look, but kept to his schedule. As the plane left the area the enormous boiling mound was seen to be beginning to subside. The copilot later checked several agencies, including the Coast Guard and the FBI, as well as seismic specialists, but received no corroborating information of anything unusual, such as earthquakes, tidal waves, or enormous waterspouts, having transpired in the area.[4]

The Montrose Harbor breakwater between Evanston, Ill., and Chicago is a pleasant, almost peaceful, place to fish. On the breakwater one can turn his back on the noise and bustle of the city and direct his attention out across this lonely miniature sea. About 50 citizens were peacefully enjoying just such a calm clear day on June 26, 1954, when a few of them noticed with dismay an eight-foot swell rising from the otherwise calm lake and moving toward them.

Some survived by clinging to the pier, while others saw the swell coming and climbed the lighthouse. Other fishermen said they saw the swell only an instant before being hit.[5]

All things considered it was a bad day for relaxing. Eight died.

The same thing happened in Holland, Mich., in 1938. It was not as serious, though. Five died.[6]

Historian Mansfield recorded the following report on Lake Ontario's odd behavior in 1872:

Phenomenon on Lake Ontario—A phenomenon of the most unusual kind occurred on Lake Ontario June 13, between 3:30 and 5 o'clock. There was but little wind, and that was from the southeast, and the surface of the lake was quite smooth. The water would rise with great rapidity by successive little swells for 15 or 20 minutes, remain stationary for a short time, then fall with the same rapid, silent, imperceptible manner. This occurred five or six times, and then remained stationary at the lowest ebb until a gale in the afternoon came up, after which it found its normal condition.[7]

The phenomenon has never been explained.

The *Sachem*[8] is a tug for the Dunbar & Sullivan firm. It is used to tow dredging equipment from one job to another and move scows around when at the dredging site.

It has an unusual history—perhaps the most unusual history of any ship afloat in this century.

On Saturday morning, December 16, 1950, the *Sachem*

took the big dipper dredge *Omadhaun* in tow at Dunkirk, N.Y. The *Omadhaun* was to be moved to Buffalo, N.Y., for the winter. It was a 37-mile trip. The *Sachem* and the *Omadhaun* arrived at Buffalo early afternoon, December 16, 1950. The trip was followed by routine weekend revelry in Buffalo. At 6:20 A.M. on Monday, December 18, the *Sachem* departed Buffalo, N.Y., with 12 aboard. She was headed southwest back to Dunkirk, N.Y. At 7:10 A.M. Capt. Irwin P. Paulson, master of the steamer *Venus*, saw the *Sachem*. The *Sachem* was making good time through the beautiful calm lake.

It was to be many months before anyone saw the *Sachem* again.

A few days later a massive search for the *Sachem* began. By December 29, 1950, all hope for survivors was scotched. The *Sachem's* only lifeboat was found. It was perfectly seaworthy. It was empty. The bodies of crewmen were recovered from the lake from January 5, 1951, through September 23, 1951.

During the search an oil slick led the Coast Guard cutter *Tupelo* to a spot just 11 miles from the *Sachem's* destination and barely two miles from shore. There, sonar quickly located a sunken ship. On January 6, 1951, the sunken ship was identified as the *Sachem*. Divers meticulously studied every detail of the vessel. On October 22, 1951, the *Sachem* was raised. What the Coast Guard investigators found was so unusual that I have been unable to find any record of a comparable event either before or since, throughout the history of world shipping.

Everything aboard the *Sachem* was in perfect order. The engine was serviceable. The steering gear still worked perfectly. The seacocks were closed as they should have been. The hull was completely undamaged. Even the instruments in the engine room were still operable. The alarm bell switch was open. The alarm had not been sounded. She was, according to the experts, a seaworthy, sunken ship. The engine controls in both the pilot house and the engine room were in the stop position, and the rudder and steering gear were in the full right position. The entire ship yielded but one clue to what sank her—

and that clue has raised more questions than it will ever answer. All the windows in the pilot house were broken out. The wind was only 14 miles per hour and there was no appreciable sea when she disappeared. Yet the bow windows were broken out and the perfectly sound *Sachem* was sunk. What could explain such circumstances? The Marine Board of Investigation did make a proposal:

> A particularly heavy wave, i.e., a "Seiche Wave"— a phenomenon wherein one large wave is unaccompanied by preceding or following waves of comparable size and not dependent upon strong winds for its formation. These waves are not unknown on the Great Lakes although recorded instances of their occurrences have been infrequent. Assuming such a wave was sighted to starboard [right], the pilot no doubt would attempt to head into it, hence the hard right position of the helm and rudder. It would also be natural to stop the engine momentarily to lessen the impact. This would explain the stopped position on the pilot house control. The fact that all the windows in the pilot house were found broken by the first divers to descend to the *Sachem*, lends credence to the aforementioned theory.[9]

In other words, a giant wave swelled from the lake surface and destroyed the *Sachem* without being noticed by any other ships or shoreside witnesses. So great was the power of this strange, inexplicable, single wave that it overcame the ship, simultaneously breaking out the windows and completely filling her with water. This occurred despite the fact that the *Sachem's* master, Capt. Hector Church, or whoever was commanding in the pilot house, had seen the horrifying sight rising toward him, stopped the engines and turned to meet the wall of water head on. Though this explanation holds faithfully to the facts of the case, it raises more awesome mysteries than it solves.

What force was behind this strange devastating wave? From where did it come? What power generated it? How could it be so accurately directed as to send a perfectly seaworthy ship crashing to the bottom and yet go completely unnoticed by everyone else on, around or above Lake Erie? The *Sachem* was only two miles from shore, yet no one on shore noticed unusual seas that day.

The board made no attempt to answer these questions. The board's explanation is every bit as impossible as the incident itself.

But the *Sachem* did sink. Her crew did perish.

If one accepts the possibility of such a strange and powerful wave, then some of the marine disasters discussed in Chapter Two become plausible.

Although it was never so officially documented, researcher Berlitz did find evidence of similar mysterious conditions within the Bermuda Triangle region of the Atlantic. The following incident was told to Berlitz by Capt. Don Henry of the *Good News* regarding a 1966 incident:

We were coming in on the return trip between Puerto Rico and Fort Lauderdale. We had been out for three days towing an empty barge which had carried petroleum nitrate. I was aboard the *Good News*, a 160-foot-long tug of 2000 horsepower. The barge we were towing weighed 2500 tons and was on a line 1000 feet behind. We were on the Tongue of the Ocean, after coming through the Exumas. The depth was about 600 fathoms [3600 feet].

It was afternoon, the weather was good, and the sky was clear. I had gone to the cabin in back of the bridge for a few minutes when I heard a lot of hollering going on. I came out of the cabin onto the bridge and yelled, "What the hell is going on?" The first thing I looked at was the compass, which was spinning clockwise. There was no reason that this should ever happen—the only place besides here I ever heard it to happen was in the St. Lawrence River at Kingston [Ont., where Lake Ontario flows into the river], where a big deposit of iron or maybe a meteorite on the bottom makes the compasses go crazy. I did not know what had happened, but something big was sure as hell going on. The water seemed to come from all directions. The horizon disappeared—we couldn't see where the horizon was—the water, sky and horizon all blended together. We couldn't see where we were.

Whatever was happening robbed, stole or borrowed everything from our generators. All electric appliances and outlets ceased to produce power. The generators were still running, but we weren't getting any power. The engineer tried to start an auxiliary generator but couldn't get a spark.

I was worried about the tow. It was tight but I couldn't see it. It seemed to be covered by a cloud, and around it the waves seemed to be more choppy than in other areas.

I rammed the throttles full ahead. I couldn't see where we were going, but I wanted to get the hell out in a hurry. It seemed that something wanted to pull us back, but it couldn't quite make it.

Coming out of it was like coming out of a fog bank. When we came out the towline was sticking out straight like the Indian rope trick—with nothing visible at the end of it where it was covered by a fog concentrated around it. I jumped to the main deck and pulled. The damned barge came out from the fog, but there was no fog anyplace else. In fact, I could see for 11 miles. In the foggy area where the tow should have been, the water was confused, although the waves were not big. Call me Nero, not Hero—I wasn't going back to find out what it was that was back there.

Have you ever felt two people pulling on your arms in opposite directions? It felt like we were on a place or point that somebody or something wanted, and somebody or something wanted us to be in another place from where we were going.[10]

Berlitz found no explanation for the incident Captain Henry described. No one is sure what kind of juggernaut is capable of turning a small spot of water into the boiling violence described in Chippewa legend. The Coast Guard calls it a "seiche" and attempts no explanation. The Chippewa call it Nanabazhoo's sturgeon and explain it as the flick of a mighty fishtail. Neither disposition is satisfactory to the mariners who have faced the danger.

But there is another important characteristic of the incident Captain Henry described. It was the way the barge disappeared before the eyes of the men on the *Good News*. This has happened many times in the Great Lakes. Such events are discussed in the next chapter.

Chapter Five:

OBSERVED DISAPPEARANCES

Reliable witnesses have watched huge ships and powerful aircraft passing nearby. Watched as the vessels passed into oblivion. Vanished.

Cleveland Tankers Incorporated, which owned barges operated by Allied Oil Transport, bought the tug *W. H. Meyer* on July 14, 1942. The *Meyer* was a 90-foot steel tug of 130 gross tons. Cleveland Tankers changed the stout ship's name to the *Admiral*.[1] As the *Admiral* her history was short. Some 89 days later she would vanish only a short distance from the southern shore of Lake Erie.

This, however, was but one small mystery in the astonishing chain of events that began on Lake Erie, before daylight on December 2, 1942.

Cleveland Tankers Inc. had bought the ship to tow their tanker barge *Clevco*.[2] Capt. John Swanson, 42, who had commanded the *Clevco*, was made master of the *Admiral*, and Swanson's former first mate, William H. Smith, 62, then became captain of the *Clevco*. The two vessels began their day on December 1, 1942, at the Sun Oil Company dock in Toledo, Ohio, where the *Clevco* was loaded with part of her 1,000,000 gallons of crude oil (one account lists the cargo as fuel oil). Later that day, while part of the crew was in downtown Toledo cashing paychecks, the *Clevco* was moved to the Gulf Refining Company's Maumee River marine terminal to finish the loading. By 2:00 P.M. both crews were aboard their respective craft and the Wheeling and Lake Erie bridge that spans the Maumee River opened to permit the tug and her consort to proceed toward the open lake.

Both vessels were properly battened down so as to maintain buoyancy. Sometime after dusk the pair turned eastward toward the dangerous Pelee Passage on the Southwest Shoals course. Eastward, safely beyond the passage, the men on the *Clevco* watched the *Admiral's* lights fade away. This puzzled but did not alarm the men. The line connecting the two vessels remained tight.

At 4:00 A.M. on December 2, the lookout on the *Clevco* noticed something even more extraordinary. The towline, which should have been pointing forward across the surface of Lake Erie, was instead running down toward the bottom of the lake. It was still tight. This was hard to believe.

The *Admiral* had in no way indicated distress. But distress signals notwithstanding, the *Admiral* was clearly no longer afloat. No one today clearly understands how such silent and devastating events are possible. No one on the *Clevco* understood either. But the 18 men of the *Clevco* sadly concluded that whatever force could do such a thing was not likely to leave survivors. Available information confirms their conclusion.

All 14 aboard the *Admiral* perished.

In an odd way, the destruction of the *Admiral* ensured the survival of the *Clevco*—or rather it would have ensured the *Clevco's* survival had it not been for another circumstance. The *Admiral*, firmly entrenched on the bottom, as all evidence indicates, would safely anchor the *Clevco* until another tug arrived. The *Clevco's* Captain Smith had to call his employers and explain that their new tug was nothing more than an excellent anchor.

Smith gave his location to the Coast Guard then as about eight miles off Avon Point, 15 miles west of Cleveland. By the time the tugs *California* and *Pennsylvania*, operated by the Great Lakes Towing Co., left Cleveland Harbor to retrieve the *Clevco,* the barge was "anchored" barely 18 miles northwest of Cleveland, according to Smith's report. Capt. L. M. Jonassen, manager of Cleveland Tankers, also notified the Coast Guard. Motor lifeboats from Lorain, Ohio, and Cleveland were dispatched, as were the Coast Guard cutters *Ossipee* and *Crocus*. They were sent to the scene quickly on the chance that survivors might have escaped the *Admiral*.

They never found where the *Admiral* disappeared.

They could not even find the *Clevco*.

Radio communication with the *Clevco* was kept open. To solve the mystery, the Civil Air Patrol began searching at dawn, using Cleveland as their base of operations. Results were quick. Civil Air Patrol pilot Clara W. Livingston spotted the barge ten miles north of Cleveland—an unbelievable 15 miles from Smith's reported position. It was no wonder rescuers had not found the *Clevco*. She was now adrift. There is no plausible explanation for this, though it is generally thought that the line was intentionally cut by Captain Smith of the *Clevco*. No one has offered suggestions on why Smith might have done this.

Rescue pilot Livingston would have directed surface craft to the *Clevco* were it not for an unusual event. A heavy cloud of snow descended upon the *Clevco* right before her eyes. When Livingston's radio failed, she did a very wise thing. She pointed her airplane south, flew for four minutes until she saw the shoreline, and followed it back to the airport. Though pilot Livingston was the first, she was by no means the only one to see the *Clevco* —and then see the *Clevco* disappear. In fact the *Clevco* vanished right before the eyes of all the would-be rescuers. And all the while she kept open radio communication with them.

There is virtually no doubt that the *Clevco* really was just ten miles from Cleveland. Once, even, the *Ossipee* got within 150 yards of the *Clevco*. The Coast Guardsmen were ready to fire lines to her. But, as before, the wily cloud of snow again quickly descended upon the *Clevco*. It was about 3:30 P.M. that the men of the *Clevco* fully appreciated the seriousness of their situation. They said they were no longer concerned about getting their barge towed to safety. They wanted to be evacuated. This unfortunately did not make their rescue possible.

No radio messages were received from the *Clevco* after 4:40 P.M.

The Coast Guard officer commanding the *Ossipee* did transmit instructions to the *Clevco*. He told her to pump oil onto the water. This, he thought, might help him locate the elusive barge. There is some evidence that these instructions were received. At daybreak—more than a day after the adventure began—the men of the *Ossipee* found two bodies, wearing *Clevco* lifejackets. Both were covered with oil. Some more bodies were found. Some were not. None of the 32 survived.

The men of the *Ossipee* were lauded for their valor. It was later learned that they had continued their search despite some frightening events aboard their own vessel. The gyro compass, a highly reliable instrument used to steer and navigate the ship, broke. The ship's steel safe was ripped loose from its fastenings, apparently without damage to any other part of the ship. And some veterans of many stormy years at sea were, at various times, suddenly afflicted with a seasickness that left others unaffected. The crew of the Coast Guard cutter *Crocus* ran into similar problems. It burst into flames. The fire was extinguished and the *Crocus* safely returned to port, but she was effectively eliminated from the mission.

No one knows how or why the *Clevco* and the *Admiral* were lost—only that they vanished on December 2, 1942, a few miles from downtown Cleveland.

High, thin cirrus is a kind of cloud usually between 20,000 and 25,000 feet above sea level. Cirrus clouds are thin enough so that the sun and moon can be seen through them. Cirrus reports mean good weather to aviators because conditions must be relatively clear for weather observers even to detect the light clouds. Such conditions prevailed over Lake Ontario on September 27, 1960, when a Canadian twin-jet interceptor, number 18469,[3] took off. Another pilot in another CF-100 was trailing the lead jet by just a few miles. Visibility was excellent, and the second pilot easily kept visual contact with the first until 18469 entered the cirrus.

There it vanished in an instant.

The airborne eyewitness's account might raise questions about his attentiveness, except that a clear white contrail (condensation trail, sometimes called vapor trail) remained for some time. It ended, but not in the normal way. The contrail was not changing altitude into warmer or drier air. The contrail didn't end in an explosion, which would leave a large cloud of smoke with streamers pointing downward. The contrail simply ended as though both engines had simultaneously flamed out. But even simultaneous failure of both engines wouldn't explain the situation. Why didn't the pilot simply explain his problem over the radio, then bail out?

Like all Canadian military aircraft accident investigations, the probable cause is classified secret. I have seen part of the classified documents. The secret is that the Canadian Defense authorities could not explain the accident.

The interceptor and its pilot remain missing.

Similarly, the Canadian Air Force was unable to assign a cause to the disappearance of another CF-100, number 18448,[4] on August 2, 1956, near the Bruce Peninsula, which divides Lake Huron from its Georgian Bay. The official description of the accident, open to public inspection, is as follows:

> The leader of a two-plane night formation out of North Bay reported that his number two had complained of vertigo, broke formation and disappeared. The aircraft and crew have not been found.

Capt. Herman Schunemann, owner and master of the *Rouse Simmons*,[5] was well known for his skills as a seaman. The big gale of 1889 had broken the masts of every schooner on Lake Michigan, except the *Rouse Simmons*. He was especially well known in the city of Chicago, even to those who knew nothing of his experience as a skipper. It was the *Rouse Simmons* that brought Chicago her Christmas trees each year. Consequently it was known to the public as the "Christmas Ship" or the "Christmas Tree Ship" or even the "Santa Claus Ship." When timber companies had left Michigan's upper peninsula, they left it bare. In place of the forest were millions of pine and balsam second-growth trees, just the right size for Chicago's Christmas trees.

With a shipload of such saplings Schunemann left Thompson Harbor just southwest of Manistique, Mich., at noon on November 25, 1913. He had sent word to Chicago that he would arrive early on November 27. But that estimate was based on an unwarranted assumption: Schunemann assumed that nothing unusual would happen aboard the *Rouse Simmons* that he as skipper could not handle. Something unusual did happen; however, historians are not sure exactly what.

At noon on November 26, the United States Lifesaving Service Station at Sturgeon Bay, Wisc., spotted the *Rouse Simmons* proceeding rapidly southward along the west shore of Lake Michigan. The *Rouse Simmons* was flying distress signals. She was making good time, and the men of the Sturgeon Bay station didn't see any hope of catching the speedy schooner that was calling for rescue. The Sturgeon Bay station notified the Kewaunee station 25 miles south. There the lifesavers headed out into the lake in one of their large surfboats. They saw the *Rouse Simmons*. Then a veil of heavy mist descended upon her. She disappeared. They continued toward her. They continued until it was apparent that the *Rouse Simmons* was no longer there.

The *Rouse Simmons* never arrived in Chicago.

She is presumed to have taken her crew—probably 17 men, though records conflict—to the bottom.

But like so many before her, the *Rouse Simmons* left but a single token of her existence. Commercial fishermen, some ten years after the disappearance, pulled up in their nets a waterlogged wallet—the wallet of Capt. Herman Schunemann.

Less credible reports were published by local newspapers on December 21, 1917, indicating the *Rouse Simmons* was still afloat, sailing Lake Michigan four years after she was presumed lost. "Patrols and sentries along the lake shore reported seeing the 'Christmas Ship' in the offing at daylight today." Then on August 20, 1919, six years after the presumed loss, newspaper readers were told of the following yet unexplained sighting:

That the hulk of an ancient ship reported by the *S.S. Carolina* to be drifting about in Lake Michigan, a few miles from Chicago, might be the ghost of the missing *Rouse Simmons*, the "Santa Claus" ship that went down in a gale in 1913, released from Davy Jones' locker by a caprice of nature was declared impossible today by Capt. John Anderson of the Coast Guard.

He is on the lookout, trying to solve the mystery of the derelict which was reported by wireless from the *Carolina* last night. The Coast Guard immediately attempted to discover the derelict, but the heavy mist hanging over the water prevented finding it.

It was then thought the wreckage might be part of the *Rouse Simmons*, the Christmas tree ship that went down off Chicago with 18 persons on board. But since seven years have elapsed, authorities pointed out that no ship would have floated about the lake without being sighted.

The disappearance of the *Rouse Simmons* is one of the most thoroughly studied disasters in the history of U.S. merchant shipping.

No one knows what happened to her.

A Piper PA-23, registration N4596P,[6] departed Merrill C. Meigs Field, Chicago, on November 29, 1960. At the controls was an experienced commercial pilot, fully instrument-rated, age 26. He carried two passengers. Shortly after takeoff he returned to Meigs and was cleared to land. He began the approach, but prior to touchdown he leveled off at 100 feet above the runway. He then advised Meigs Tower that he would "go around," which meant he was beginning another approach. This is not as unusual as it may seem to those unfamiliar with aircraft operations. Many an airline passenger has done it without realizing it. But what happened next to N4596P is extraordinary. He started a right turn away from downtown Chicago and out toward Lake Michigan. As he turned, he disappeared. Air traffic controllers in the tower said a snowy cloud enveloped N4596P. No further radio communications were received.

N4596P has not been seen since.

Colpoys Bay is on the east side of the Bruce Peninsula. It opens into Georgian Bay of Lake Huron. In 1881, Roderick Cameron and his son lived on the south side of the bay a few miles from Wiarton, Ont. And on November 25, 1881, they were keeping a close watch from the windows of their home. They were expecting the *Wiarton Belle*, on which another of the Cameron sons was to arrive. By watching for the *Wiarton Belle*, they would see it in time to go to Wiarton and pick him up as the ship docked.

History has recorded little about the *Wiarton Belle* that night, but Cameron and his son did see something of historical significance. It was the *Jane Miller*,[7] a small passenger steamer. She was about a half mile offshore. She was apparently headed for Wiarton too. Cameron later recalled how curious it was that the ship seemed so stationary. She was not sounding any signal of distress. She remained afloat. A heavy cloud completely enveloped the ship, making it impossible to see her. The cloud quickly lifted.

The *Jane Miller* was no longer there.

Cameron was puzzled but not alarmed. It seemed more plausible that the ship had charged away under cover of the strange cloud than that she could have sunk in such a short time. Few details can be concluded from the Camerons' observation beyond what one historian reported, that "the *Jane Miller* simply vanished in the comparatively quiet waters of Colpoys Bay."

The bay was searched and the bottom combed with grapnels. No bodies and no ship were found. The 28 aboard are presumed to have perished. The absence of bodies is unexplained. Rescuers did find one scrap of evidence attributable to the *Jane Miller's* passage.

Five uniform caps belonging to crew members were found floating where Cameron saw the ship vanish.

United Airlines Flight 314,[8] a Convair 340, departed Chicago Midway Airport at 6:58 P.M. on August 26, 1953. Its destination was Cleveland, Ohio. At the controls were Capt. Lewis M. Brubaker, a 32-year-old airline transport pilot with more than 6000 hours' experience, and copilot Charles E. Olsen, 28.

American Airlines Flight 714,[9] a Convair 240, departed Chicago Midway about two minutes after United 314. American 714's destination was Ypsilanti, Mich. At the controls was Capt. Dwight W. Davison, 37, a ten-year veteran of American Airlines with more than 5000 hours' experience. His copilot was William M. Haag, Jr., 28, who had more than 3000 hours' experience.

Both aircraft planned to use 11,000 feet as their enroute altitude. At 10,800 feet, near the southeast corner of Lake Michigan, the two airliners collided. American 714 returned to Midway. United 314 landed at South Bend, Ind. No one was injured.

Detailed investigation reconstructed both flights from start to finish. There had been some light haze at lower altitudes, but both pilots climbed out of the top of the haze at about 9000 or 10,000 feet. Above the haze, the sky was clear and visibility was unlimited—unlimited at least in the conventional sense of the word. The airliners did collide. Captain Brubaker of the United flight later said that he saw nothing, that he glanced down into the cockpit to make some adjustments on the controls, and that when he looked back up American 714 filled his windshield. This is particularly astonishing in light of the fact that their respective speeds were probably well under 30 miles per hour. Newspapers made an odd speculation about the reason for the accident:

> Questioning of both crews brought out the fact that the huge full moon of that evening which was shining with almost daylight brightness also played a part in the near-tragedy. Both crews reported that although the weather was perfect and the sky cloudless, the moon, in the east, poured into the cockpits and dazzled crew eyes.

The Civil Aeronautics Board took a somewhat more conservative approach to the question of moon-bedazzled pilots. They ignored it. The Civil Aeronautics Board did make a number of observations pertinent to the accident.

The most concise was that "All of the pilots should have been able to see the other aircraft . . . [well before the crash]."

None did.

The National Transportation Safety Board, successor to the Civil Aeronautics Board, made the same determination when two airline flights ended simultaneously over Lake Winnebago in a midair collision on June 29, 1972. Lake Winnebago is just west of Lake Michigan and south of Green Bay. The North Central Airlines Convair 580, N98858,[10] was on its way from Green Bay, Wisc., to Chicago. The Air Wisconsin DeHavilland DHC-6, N40438,[11] was on its way from Chicago to Appleton, Wisc. Weather was good. Both aircraft sank in Lake Winnebago. All pilots should have seen the imminent disaster in plenty of time to avoid the collision. None did.

As a result all four pilots and all passengers died.

The North Central Flight, it seems, although operating legally, was ten miles off the most plausible route between Green Bay and Chicago. No one knows why.

Lansing, Mich., is surrounded by Lake Huron, Lake Michigan and Lake Erie. High above Lansing on the night of March 18, 1960, Capt. W. H. Smith and copilot David M. Monroe were at the controls of Northwest Airlines Flight 7[12] from New York City Idlewild Airport to Minneapolis. There, over Lansing, they saw approaching out of the darkness from their left, heading toward Lake Huron, a close formation of aircraft navigation lights. According to both pilots, the aircraft lights from more than one aircraft remained fixed on the windshield, growing larger. This meant that the Northwest Airlines Boeing 377 and the lights were on converging courses. Smith took evasive action, which injured one passenger. The accident was *not* Smith's fault. Smith told me recently that the lights never altered their course.

"It was as though they couldn't see us," he said.

Important factors common to the near-miss of Northwest 7 and each of the previously discussed collisions are the clear weather and the fact that the aircraft were never approaching on opposite courses. (The Lake Winnebago case may be an exception to the second characteristic.) When high-speed aircraft are speeding through limited visibility, constant pilot vigilance to avoid collisions is necessary. Approaching head-on through visibility limited to just a few miles can leave a pilot with only a few seconds to avoid a collision. But in these cases pilots had at least several seconds and probably several minutes in which to see and avoid the accidents that should have been frighteningly apparent.

The *Cyprus*[18] was the fifth of six big steel freighters, all exactly alike, built in Lorain, Ohio. It was launched September 17, 1907. The other five sister ships have enjoyed a long career on the Great Lakes. By the end of September the *Cyprus* had delivered her first cargo of iron ore to Fairport, Ohio. She returned to Superior, Wisc., for the second cargo of her life, 7103 tons of iron ore.

With the load, she left the harbor Wednesday morning, October 9. Her journey continued as planned until Thursday after dusk as she neared a place on Lake Superior where many ships, including the *Edmund Fitzgerald*, have vanished.

Like the *Fitzgerald*, the *Cyprus* picked up a companion along the way. Only a short distance from the *Cyprus* was the freighter *George Stephenson*. The crew later reported what they saw:

It gave them a comfortable feeling in the storm. Suddenly the comfortable feeling was gone. The men in the pilot house of the *Stephenson* stared and rubbed their eyes. The lights of the *Cyprus* had disappeared. The big steel ship was blotted off the lake. [Ratigan]

There was a notable difference between the *Fitzgerald* (Chapter One) and the *Cyprus*. Somehow, when the *Cyprus* was pulled under, second mate Charles Pitz was thrown free. At daylight the U.S. Life Saving Service found Pitz lashed to a liferaft and still alive. At first it appeared the mystery of the disappearance would be concluded. But Pitz could never explain why he was alive. He was "so far gone with shock and exposure that he barely knew the name of his ship," wrote historian William Ratigan.

With the astounding number of these strange disappearances, it was not surprising that one of the most extraordinary and astonishing was witnessed by distinguished Great Lakes historian Rowley W. Murphy himself. It occurred in August 1910. Murphy's account was published by the Great Lakes Historial Society. It is included here as the final example in this chapter of a kind of occurrence that is almost unique to the Great Lakes:

> My father, a cousin, and I were on a holiday cruise around the west end of Lake Ontario, and as we were late getting underway from Toronto Island, and were running before a light easterly, decided to spend the night in the quiet sheltered and beautiful basin at the mouth of the creek spelled "Etobicoke". . . but always pronounced "Tobyco" by old-timers.
>
> Our cruising yawl, with a larger sister of the same rig and a still larger Mackinaw, were the only occupants of the harbour this perfect night. The crews of the three yachts numbered 11 in all, and as is generally the case, after dinner was over and dishes done, gathered on deck in the moonlight to engage in the best conversation known to man.
>
> All hands turned in earlier than usual, there being no distractions ashore, and by midnight were deep in happy dreams, helped by the quiet ripple alongside. At what was about 1:30 A.M. the writer [Murphy] was awakened by four blasts on a steamer's whistle [distress signal]. After waiting for a repetition . . . to be sure it was not part of a dream . . . he [Murphy] put his head out of the companionway.
>
> There, flooded by moonlight, was a steamer heading about west-southwest . . . at about half speed, and approximately half a mile off shore. She had a good chime whistle but not much steam . . . like *Noronic* on that awful night of September 17, 1949, who also repeated her four blasts many times.

65

But who was she? On this amazingly beautiful night, with memory strained to the utmost, it was difficult to do more than think of who she was not! She was considerably smaller than the three famous Upper Lakers, *China, India* and *Japan*. She was not as small as *Lake Michigan*, but like her, did appear to be of all wooden construction. However, there were many in the past, of quite related design and size. The vessel seen had white topsides and deckhouses, and appeared to be grey below her main deck, like the Welland Canal-sized freighters *Persia* and *Ocean*, were like her in size arrangement, but were all white and came to known ends, and of course, *Arabian* was of iron, and was black.

In this appearance of Etobicoke, the starboard light, deck lights and some seen through cabin windows, had the quality of oil lamps; and her tall mast, with fitted topmast, carried a gaff and brailed up mainsail. Her smokestack was all black, and she had no hog beams . . . but appeared to have four white boats. Her chime whistle was a good one, but was reduced in volume as previously mentioned and was sounded continuously for perhaps ten minutes. Very soon all hands now watching on the beach decided that something should be done. So a dinghy was quickly hauled over from the basin, and, with a crew of four made up from some of those aboard the three yachts, started to row out with all speed to the vessel in distress, to give her what assistance might be possible.

As the boys in the dinghy reached the area where something definite should have been seen, there was nothing there beyond clear and powerful moonlight, a few gulls wakened from sleep . . . but something else, impossible to ignore. This was a succession of long curving ripples in a more or less circular pattern, which just might have been the last appearance of those caused by the foundering of a steamer many years before on a night of similar beauty. In any case, the four in the dinghy returned in about an hour, reporting also small scraps of wreckage which were probably just old driftwood, seldom seen with any fresh breezes blowing.

But something more was there. This was the reappearance to the visual and audible memory, which to those on the beach and those afloat had seen and heard, of something that occurred in the more or less distant past, and which had returned to the consciousness of living men after a long absence.

Whatever the cause, the experienced crews of the three yachts mentioned were of one mind as to what they had seen and heard. At least 11 lake sailors would be unlikely to agree on the character of this reappearance without good reason! And the reason was certainly not firewater working on the mass imagination, as no one of the three yachts had any aboard. So what was the answer?[14]

Chapter Six:

IMPOSSIBLE ENGINE FAILURES

Air regulations in the United States and Canada require adherence to stringent aircraft-engine maintenance standards. Beyond this, the simplest aircraft engine has backup fuel-supply systems, backup magneto systems, backup induction systems—there are even two sparkplugs in every cylinder head. Only the most catastrophic kind of component failure can render an aircraft engine inoperative. Such failures are almost always apparent on subsequent examination.

Aircraft overflying the Great Lakes lose power with alarming frequency.

Subsequent recovery and examination show no component failures.

The contradictions are unexplained.

In 1968 what was to become a classic blues song, "Sitting on the Dock of the Bay," was released. The artist, Otis Redding, never knew of his fantastic success. Redding and his company on the afternoon of December 10, 1967, tried to fly from Cleveland to Madison, Wisc., across two of the Great Lakes, Erie and Michigan. They almost made it.

Redding's aircraft was N39OR,[1] a powerful multi-engine Beech H-18 with specially requested registration numbers ending in Redding's initials. Redding's pilot was a highly rated flight instructor, Richard P. Fraser, who had begun working for Redding six months earlier. Edson W. Beatty, the man who had given pilot Fraser his last checkride, said of the 26-year-old professional, "I was very impressed with Mr. Fraser's ability and competence."

Fraser made his weight and balance calculations,

checked the weather, filed his flight plan and had N39OR fueled before his departure at Cleveland Hopkins Airport, 2:09 P.M., December 10, 1967—the last day of his life.

About 45 minutes after takeoff, Fraser reported to Cleveland Center, "At 10,000, we've got snow with outside temperature of zero minus seven." Fifteen minutes later Cleveland Center asked if there was turbulence. Fraser replied, "Negative smooth." At 3:04 P.M., N39OR neared Lake Michigan. Cleveland Center passed it to Chicago Center. Within Chicago Center, N39OR was handed from controller to controller as it neared its destination, Madison, Wisc.

The Chicago Center controller who was handling the Milwaukee Sector gave N39OR radar vectors to Madison and told Fraser to expect an Instrument Landing System approach to runway 36 at Madison, where low ceilings were reported.

The Instrument Landing System is a very normal kind of precision approach, and Chicago Center's early advice on which approach to expect gave Fraser plenty of time to prepare himself. At just after 3:00 P.M. (N39OR had gained an hour flying west), that controller passed N39OR to the Chicago Center controller who was handling the Madison Sector.

At 3:22 P.M., N39OR was cleared for the approach, and two minutes later Chicago Center handed the flight off to the airport control tower. The tower controller reports what came next:

At approximately 1523 [3:23 P.M.], N39OR called the tower and reported on the localizer course inbound. [This meant Fraser had begun the approach.] I gave N39OR the winds, runway, and instructed him to report the marker. At 1525 [3:25 P.M.], N39OR reported the marker. [This meant Fraser was about five miles from the threshold of the runway.] I cleared him to land and turned up the approach lights and the sequence flashers. At this time, I attempted contact, but received no reply. I tried again, this time transmitting on localizer voice. Still no reply. Emergency equipment and city police were then notified.

N390R crashed into Lake Monona, killing Fraser, Redding, James King, Carl Cunningham, Phalen Jones, Matthew Kelly and Ronald Caldwell. Ben Cauley of Gray, Ga., survived. He does not know how. N39OR should have been almost 1000 feet above Lake Monona at the point where it crashed.

From the five witnesses near the edge of Lake Monona and thorough examination of the wreckage, accident investigators were able to determine that N39OR probably suffered some kind of engine trouble. Further, it is reasonable to assume that the engine trouble was serious, since Fraser ordinarily could have completed his approach easily on one engine. But as with so many other crashes in this region, subsequent examination of the wreckage revealed *no reason* for engine failure. All engine components were as they should be for normal operation.

Another irregularity so common to Great Lakes disasters was the absence of any distress call. Fraser already had an open channel to Madison Tower, and the tower operator knew his precise position. How long could it have taken Fraser to pick up his microphone, key the transmitter and say "Niner Zero Romeo, Mayday?" Perhaps two seconds. Certainly no more than three. He had plenty of time. The mystery of Otis Redding's death lingers on just like his haunting melody of a weary traveler from Georgia who relaxes his life away, "sitting on the dock of the bay."

Official cause of this accident remains "miscellaneous: undetermined," according to the National Transportation Safety Board.

When U.S. or Canadian authorities fail to find the cause of what is otherwise an apparent aircraft engine failure, they consider only the more orthodox possibilities, like fuel starvation or engine-component failure. On the other hand, astronomer Joseph Allen Hynek, in discussing many of these Great Lakes accidents with me, suggested the engine failures were consistent with vehicles known to have come in proximity with UFOs. In his book

70

on the subject, Hynek describes the phenomenon as follows:

Perhaps the most intriguing—and certainly one of the most difficult to explain in terms of our present knowledge of the physical world—are the globally reported cases in which a UFO is said to have interfered with moving automobiles by killing a car engine, extinguishing the lights, etc.

Why this physical effect, of all things? There would seem to be so many other more significant ways in which UFOs could interfere in human affairs! Yet this is what is reported: cars are seemingly accosted on lonely roads sometimes but not always resulting in a killed engine and the failure of lights and radio. It would almost seem as if the UFO regarded the cars as creatures to be investigated. This is the impression one gets from interrogation of observers and from a study of their reports. But ours is not to ask why (at least not until we have more facts); we examine what has been reported, choosing reports from those who seem to be the most credible witnesses.[2]

Hynek cites several examples and begins with one he considers most typical. It was April 3, 1968, 8:10 P.M., at Cochran, Wisc., south of Lake Superior and west of Lake Michigan. A schoolteacher and former Air Force stewardess, one of two witnesses, described the event:

. . . that thing came from the dip in the hill, real fast, but real, real smooth like something gliding, but lower than any plane, and hovered and stopped above that car [a car that had just previously passed the observer's car]. Then is when its [the other car's] lights went out, and I pulled onto the gravel because I thought it was a kid. He put out his lights, and I didn't want to smash into him—at all of this my lights were dimming slightly, but I didn't think anything of it until my engine, lights and radio went out and stopped. This happened to me when it [the UFO] left that car and came down the highway . . . and was above us. It came down over from the other car. It was pretty low. When I looked out of my windshield I had to bend forward toward the wheel, and I looked straight up and there it was above us—with the car dead. I had opened the window when the other car's lights went out, and it was open then—and absolutely no sound.[3]

Hynek reports a number of similar examples. In each case the engine suffers no apparent damage. It restarts and runs normally immediately after the UFO encounter.

How such an encounter might affect an aircraft in flight is obvious. When an airplane power plant fails, the consequences are ordinarily far more serious than one would expect when an automobile engine fails. If the aircraft-engine failures illustrated by the examples in this chapter were related to UFOs, the engine failures themselves would eliminate many possible witnesses. But even in cases where pilots land safely after engine failure, it is unlikely that they could answer resulting official inquiries about UFOs that they may or may not have seen. In most situations, the pilots are too stunned. Sometimes, the pilots do not believe what they think they saw. I for one would have no trouble in deciding my preference. I would say nothing.

On February 29, 1964, N5608P[4] departed Detroit, between Lake Huron and Lake Erie. A short time thereafter it crashed, killing one passenger and seriously injuring the pilot and remaining passenger. The official synopsis is as follows:

Several witnesses heard what they described as engine backfire or misfire followed by a power loss. When they subsequently observed the aircraft, the landing gear was being extended and a steep left turn was initiated. The aircraft then descended in a steep nosedown angle to the ground.

Inspection of the engine disclosed no mechanical reason for any malfunction or failure. The fuel tanks were full and the fuel selector was positioned on the left tank. No contamination of the fuel was found, and a cause of the power loss could not be determined. No information could be obtained from the pilot because of his injuries. The surviving passenger stated that the pilot conducted a long pre-takeoff runup and, when the backfiring occurred, the pilot said that he was going back to the airport. Weather was not a factor.

Probable Cause: Power loss . . . for an undetermined reason.

On June 5, 1960, near Brown Hill, Ont., between Georgian Bay and Lake Ontario, CF-LUE,[5] a Champion 7EC, crashed and seriously injured the pilot and his instructor. Kenneth Charles McIntosh had been practicing forced landings with instructor William Gerald Avison, a highly experienced airline transport pilot. Forced landings are a kind of emergency for which pilots are routinely trained. Instructor Avison pulled the throttle back to the idle position and applied carburetor heat. This brought the engine to an idle and pilot McIntosh was to pretend that his engine had failed. Normally the pilot practicing the forced landing picks a field and initiates his approach. When it becomes apparent that he has either judged his approach correctly or incorrectly, the throttle is advanced and the exercise is ended without ever actually descending close to the field.

Everything went as usual for CF-LUE that day until the throttle was advanced. Nothing happened. The propeller continued to windmill idly, and what had been only a practice emergency suddenly became the real thing. The field was not suitable for an actual landing and the airplane was destroyed.

Subsequent examination failed to explain the engine's behavior, and the probable cause went down as power failure for undetermined reasons.

On March 13, 1960, a few miles from the north shore of Lake Superior at Isabella, Minn., a private pilot was practicing touch-and-go landings in N48337[6] when his engine failed. The pilot was unable to turn back to the field. The plane crashed, and he died. The Civil Aeronautics Board report on the accident is as follows:

The power failure was confirmed by evidence which showed the propeller was not turning at impact; however, examination of the engine failed to disclose evidence of malfunction or failure.

73

Probable Cause: A power failure for unknown reasons.

There is an important distinction between the tragedies reported here and a much more common kind of power failure. I have experienced a number of partial or total power failures that were only temporary since they were caused by such correctable problems as carburetor ice, magneto failure or simply running a fuel tank dry. These are not considered serious problems. I have also had two engine failures permanent enough to necessitate forced landings. One resulted from a complete carburetor failure and the other was caused when a loose sparkplug exploded out of a cylinder head.

The most important difference between these power failures and the ones reported in this chapter is that no explanation exists for the accidents cited for the Great Lakes.

Another important difference between, say, my power failures and those reported in this chapter is that in my case no accident resulted. Most power failures end in a forced landing that leaves airplane and occupants undamaged. No record is kept of these events. Since research for this book came from *accident* files, there is no way to know how many Great Lakes pilots have suffered power-plant failures for no apparent reasons, landed at a convenient field, restarted the engines, and taken off, wondering who would ever believe it. Regardless of whether they told anyone or not, the occurrence would not show up in the files which contributed to this chapter.

One file that did show up is particularly mysterious because the engine failure itself should not have caused an accident. An accident nevertheless occurred near Markham, Ill., a suburb of Chicago, on September 6, 1964. Everyone involved died. The official report is as follows:[7]

At 1437 [2:37 P.M.] cst, the pilot/co-owner of N1252P [a twin-engine Piper PA-23] with a friend and the friend's wife made a normal takeoff from the southwest runway at Howell Airport. At takeoff, the friend occupied the right rear seat, his wife occupied the left seat pilot's position. All occupants were rated airplane pilots and all except the right front seat pilot were multi-engine rated. The intended purpose of the flight is not known.

About two minutes after it took off, the aircraft was observed on a southerly heading 3¾ miles southeast of Howell Airport. Witnesses stated that it was flying in a crabbed attitude 300 to 600 feet above the terrain. They said that one engine seemed to be misfiring while the other was "being gunned" [operated at high power]. They said as they watched the aircraft the landing gear extended and a left turn was initiated. During this turn the nose pitched downward to a near-vertical attitude and the aircraft crashed on wooded terrain about four miles southeast of Howell Airport. The aircraft received destructive impact damage but fire did not occur.

Investigation at the accident scene and examination of the wreckage, to the extent possible, failed to disclose any evidence of preimpact mechanical failure or malfunction.

A teardown inspection of both engines and a laboratory analysis of combustion deposits found in the cylinders was made. No evidence of any preimpact mechanical failure or malfunction that would have caused power failure was found.

The other co-owner of N1252P flew the aircraft on the flight preceding the accident flight. He stated that, to the best of his knowledge, N1252P was in perfect condition and was adequately fueled for this flight.

Post-mortem examination of the pilot did not disclose any human factor conditions pertinent to the cause of the accident.

Probable cause: A loss of power for undetermined reason, resulting in a loss of control.

Why did N1252P lose an engine? That question notwithstanding, why didn't N1252P simply continue the flight to a safe landing back at Howell airport? Why lower the gear as if an immediate landing were necessary? For that matter, why didn't Otis Redding's pilot continue his approach to a safe landing? I do not know the answers. But whatever affected one engine must have at least partially affected some other part of the airplane or crew.

Readers who are knowledgeable about aircraft and who have studied similar accidents may wonder if in the accidents cited here the pilots, faced with one engine failure, may have hastily and mistakenly feathered the remaining good engine. This is a fairly common and often fatal mistake. For those who might wonder that, the answer is clear. This is not possible. When this does happen, it is apparent to an experienced accident investigator within a few minutes after he first sees the wreckage.

N2678B[8] was a big Aero Commander on its way from Buffalo to Detroit on the afternoon of December 8, 1956. The course was straight along the north shore of Lake Erie through southern Ontario. This meant that even though N2678B was a U.S.-registered aircraft en route from one U.S. airport to another, the five bodies, the wreckage and the investigation were disposed of by the Canadian authorities. About 15 minutes after departure the pilot of N2678B

> contacted Buffalo radio reporting that he was losing an engine, losing altitude and returning to Buffalo. Clearance to return to Buffalo was transmitted and the reply received from the pilot at 1639 hours [4:39 P.M.] was that he was losing altitude rapidly and having difficulty in remaining airborne. This was the last contact with the aircraft.

Five witnesses watched N2678B struggling to stay airborne. Three of the five reported that they heard an aircraft backfiring. (An Aero Commander flies nicely on one engine, even at gross weight.) The pilot of N2678B was an airline transport pilot with 4000 hours' experience. Canadian authorities disassembled the engine and tested its components one by one. Their report ends as follows:

> Conclusions: Due to the loss of power, for reasons which were not determined and consequent loss of altitude, the aircraft crash landed on the water of Lake Erie.

A Cessna 320 has two engines. Each has six cylinders. After N9212U[9] crashed December 4, 1972, in an attempt to fly west from the east shore of Lake Michigan, authorities made a thorough examination of the wreckage. They found that the number-three cylinder ring on one engine was damaged. This caused oil to foul the sparkplugs in that one cylinder (there are two plugs in each cylinder of an aircraft engine) so that one cylinder may not have been firing properly. In other words, they found an explanation for a partial power loss on one engine. If that partial power loss really bothered the pilot at all, he could have completely shut down the weak engine and continued his flight to Arizona on one engine. That did not happen.

He died instead.

The National Transportation Safety Board lists the partial power failure as probable cause of the accident. I have considerable doubt about this explanation.

The Rev. Charles L. Upchurch and the Rev. John H. Fore were men of God. Upchurch was also a pilot. Along with Ronald E. Carter and Miss Mae Edyth Sherell, they headed across Lake Michigan on April 4, 1970, with what they thought was enough faith to see them to the Gary, Ind., airport a short distance to the southwest. Near their destination, their Beech 36, registration N7757R,[10] suffered a partial power failure. They began a long radio conversation as they gradually lost altitude over Lake Michigan. They almost made it to Gary Airport. Faith notwithstanding, they flew instead into a concrete pumphouse of the Georgia Pacific Paper Company.

All four were killed.

The National Transportation Safety Board delved into N7757R's engine. What they found was recorded as follows: "Probable Cause: Miscellaneous: Powerplant failure for undetermined reasons."

That was precisely the same nonexplanation for the crash of N9356T[11] at Whitmore Lake, Mich., on June

12, 1971. Whitmore Lake is about ten miles north of Ann Arbor just west of Detroit, and N9356T was a Cessna 180. Aeronautically the only other difference between the crash of N9356T and of Rev. Upchurch's N7757R was that in the case of N9356T, the power failure was complete.

The pilot and two passengers were killed.

On February 16, 1972, N80398,[12] a Beech 18, much like Otis Redding's airplane, was on its way from Chicago, Ill., to Detroit, Mich. That is across Lake Michigan—close to where Redding crossed. N80398 made it as far as Jackson, Mich., where it crashed and all on board were killed. Like Redding's plane, it apparently suffered total power loss on one engine and partial power loss on the other. Also like its more famous predecessor, the authorities were not able to offer any explanation for the power failure. In the case of N80398, the pilot was airline-transport-rated and thoroughly experienced. Weather at the accident site was good.

Government files similarly describe the trip of a 29-year-old flight instructor with more than 1000 hours in Piper PA-28s like N6678W,[13] the one that killed him on June 17, 1969.

On a routine flight with a student aboard, his engine failed after takeoff from Grayslake, Ill., a few miles north of Chicago just off the west shore of Lake Michigan. The flight instructor then for some unexplained reason stalled the airplane and plummeted to the ground. It's unlikely that a professional flight instructor with more than 1000 hours in PA-28s could accidentally stall a Piper with or without an operating engine. This flight instructor certainly had given at least 100 hours' instruction, if not several hundred hours' instruction, in stalls. What is even more puzzling is why an aircraft engine would stop for no reason. Nevertheless, the probable cause of the accident was "miscellaneous: powerplant failure for undetermined reasons." The instructor missed the deadline for being listed as a fatality in his own crash. He lived for ten days, and therefore according to government records he was only "seriously injured." The student easily made the deadline and was duly recorded as a fatality.

A 27-year-old commercial instructor pilot died alone and promptly when he crashed his Cessna 140, N2385V,[14] just after takeoff on September 23, 1960. His unplanned arrival was near Muskego, Wisc., just south of Milwaukee on the west shore of Lake Michigan. As in the other cases, subsequent disassembly of the engine revealed no cause for a power failure. There is one interesting addition to this accident. It occurred at night, and the pilot had his navigation lights on. Pilots who saw the plane just before it crashed reported the following observation:

> Pilot witnesses said that shortly after takeoff the navigation lights of the aircraft went out and the engine sound diminished more rapidly than that attributable to the aircraft moving away from them.

This is odd because the navigation lights are not dependent on the engine, and the engine is not dependent on the electrical system (unlike an automobile). What could have simultaneously doused the navigation lights and slowly robbed the engine of its power?

No explanation can be given.

Another of the rare failures by crash investigators came in their search for a cause to the April 1, 1965, crash of N3600D,[15] a multi-engine Cessna 310, near Blissfield, Mich., which is near Toledo, Ohio, on the west end of Lake Erie. At 3:00 P.M. that day, a highly experienced 42-year-old commercial pilot left Adrian, Mich., not far from Toledo, and headed home to Lockport, Ill.

> Shortly after the aircraft was airborne, the pilot radioed he was experiencing a propeller malfunction and he requested and received an emergency . . . clearance to the Toledo, Ohio, Express Airport.

It was about this time that a witness on the ground,

a pilot himself, heard and recognized a propeller-overspeed sound, and saw N3600D over the Adrian airport. A few minutes later, the pilot radioed that his left engine had failed. And with that same transmission the pilot said two other very curious things. He said he was unable to hold his altitude and that all his radio navigation equipment had failed. Radar continued to receive a nice bright return from N3600D for another four minutes, whereupon that disappeared.

The pilot and his only passenger were killed in the crash.

Accident investigators quickly disassembled the left propeller governor and immediately identified the problem originally reported by the pilot. A small broken screw had caused the propeller to overspeed and at the same time prevented it from feathering properly. But the pilot's subsequent report of an engine failure was not verified.

In fact, breakdown of both engines showed no pre-impact failure of either one. The only thing wrong with either engine was minor impact damage. A propeller overspeed is only a problem because it allows the engine to overrev, and this can lead to rapid engine wear. But even if there was something wrong with the left engine, which is contradicted by the subsequent examination, N3600D should have been able to continue even with one propeller unfeathered. It was lightly loaded. The right engine should easily have kept it aloft.

There were other mysteries involving the crash of N3600D. For one, the aircraft, cleared to Toledo Express Airport, was not headed in that direction. From where the ground witness saw N3600D at Adrian to the crash site is almost due east. From Adrian to Toledo Express Airport is southeast.

The failure of the navigation radios is also peculiar. There are various stages of lost radio reception, but the weakest of signals will give a needle indication on navigation radios like those in N3600D. As an aircraft descends, these needle indications are usually the last radio reception lost. Primary radar contact is usually the first to be lost. In this case the ground-based communication station and the radar antenna were both slightly closer to N3600D than was the ground-based radio navigation antenna. Still, it is unclear how the pilot lost total radio navigation indication while he was still clearly audible to Toledo Approach and still clearly visible on primary radar.

The same thing happened under even more incredible circumstances in 1951. That strange incident is described at the beginning of the next chapter.

Chapter Seven:

EFFECTS ON RADIOS

Avionics, which include a broad spectrum of radio-like equipment, are used by aircraft for navigation and communication. Something, somewhere, from time to time and for no apparent reason, affects normal avionics operation in the Great Lakes. Whether this something alters the characteristics of electromagnetic wave propagation, or the circuitry of the airborne or ground-based equipment, or whether it affects the minds of the pilots and/or air controllers is not known.

At 3:00 A.M. on December 20, 1951, a Curtis C-46E airliner, N59487,[1] took off from Chicago Airport and ascended into the clouds. Aboard were two pilots, one stewardess, 42 adult passengers and two infants. They were planning to fly direct to Newark, N.J. The planned course would have taken them across the southern tip of Lake Michigan and along the southern shoreline of western Lake Erie.

Something altered the intended course.

Climbing out of Chicago, N59487 quickly reached its assigned altitude, 9000 feet, and Capt. B. E. Smelser leveled off on his planned route eastward. He reported positions over South Bend, Goshen, and Toledo, all as planned. The weather was dreary that morning before first light. Flying through the solid overcast, no one aboard N59487 had glimpsed the earth's surface since they left Chicago. Because of the hour and the weather, N59487 was almost alone in the sky that covers Toledo.

But the 44 passengers were in experienced hands. Captain Smelser had more than 10,000 hours at the controls, 3000 hours at the controls of the Curtis C-46E.

Copilot E. T. O'Leary had almost as much experience. Also he had shown particular attention to planning this flight. It was to be his eastern route check.

After Toledo, N59487's next checkpoint was Cleveland. The airliner was skirting the southern edge of Lake Erie. But something peculiar happened to the avionics aboard N59487 that morning. They did not receive Cleveland's navigational transmitters. For that matter, they did not receive navigational information from anywhere. Try as they did, their communication transmissions went unanswered. The pilots tried to tune in continuous weather broadcasts. Nothing. The radios aboard N59487 produced no evidence that anyone else in the world existed. Alone, speeding through the high, misty overcast, the 47 souls inside N59487 were as alone that dawn as anyone could be. No one on the ground or in the air knew it, but the C-46E was not traveling southeastward. Those aboard the airliner were being carried northeastward over Lake Erie toward Lake Ontario. Whether it was a strange and powerful steady wind carrying them northward or whether something altered the compasses in the cockpit, the two pilots had no way of knowing.

As the clock ticked on, Cleveland's mysterious absence became more and more disturbing. Finally the pilots knew they must be near Cleveland, so they began flying different courses trying to receive Cleveland. Efforts were futile. The radios were useless. The only alternative was to proceed on course, hoping that either the problem with the radios would correct itself, or N59487 would break out of the clouds, allowing the flight to proceed visually. But N59487 did not break out. The situation grew more critical with each passing minute. The pilots calculated and recalculated their fuel-exhaustion time. If they waited until the engines ran dry while they were still in the clouds, they would probably kill everyone aboard, including themselves. If they began a descent through the clouds, they ran the risk of flying blind into a mountain. In addition, the lower altitudes would burn away their fuel more quickly. The best chance for survival was to wait until the last minute, then begin the dangerous descent while there was still just enough fuel to find a suitable place for an emergency landing. The radios remained silent. The pilots adjusted their engines to power settings somewhere between maximum endurance and maximum range. Then they calculated with growing concern what would be the exact minute of fuel exhaustion. Still they were cloaked in the overcast. They had seen nothing but themselves, their airplane and the white mist that surrounded them since leaving Chicago.

Their tension grew as their fuel supply diminished. A small mistake in arithmetic or in reading numbers from a table and the engines might stop several minutes before anticipated. Still the radios were silent. Finally they had no choice. They acted in accordance with reason. They began the dangerous descent. They didn't know where they were and they hadn't set their altimeters for some time. The prospect of slamming into the side of a mountain grew with every foot below 6000. Below that point, a steep rapid descent was safer than a slow shallow one. They must have pushed the yoke forward. The nose pointed down toward whatever lay ahead. Faced with instant death, the assurance of living a few minutes longer is a tremendous relief. Though fuel was almost gone, both pilots could take a deep breath when they broke out of the clouds. They could see for miles. What they saw was not reassuring—an expanse of open water. It was Lake Ontario, but for all Smelser and O'Leary knew it could have been the Atlantic Ocean.

Then a most peculiar thing happened. Suddenly their silent radios began reporting from Rochester, N.Y. Rochester had the flight on radar. N59487 was on the Canadian side of Lake Ontario. Smelser explained what had happened thus far. Rochester gave N59487 a heading that would bring it back to Rochester. As Rochester was transmitting this information the left engine ran dry. There was no longer any possibility of mistake in computing the fuel-exhaustion time. The right engine would soon follow the example of the left and N59487 would become a very heavy glider. Smelser turned north, trying to make the closest land with his one good engine. There ahead lay the northern shoreline of Lake Ontario. As the airplane crossed it, the right engine stopped. Captain Smelser left the landing gear up in the retracted position. A landing gear that breaks on a rough field can cause an airplane to yaw and flip, and Smelser knew that if the airplane inverted most of his passengers would die that day. He headed for an open snow-covered field and brought the smooth belly of his C-46E down against it.

The skin on the underside of the belly was damaged; so were both propellers and the engine nacelles. There was no other damage.

No one was injured.

The official probable cause of the accident was fuel exhaustion.

Whatever happened to the radios aboard N59487 could not be explained by experts at the time. It has not been explained since.

N151U,[2] a Beech C-45H, on December 17, 1963, had at the controls an experienced commercial pilot when it departed Buffalo, heading over Lake Erie to Cleveland. Shortly after departure about 7:30 P.M., Buffalo Radar Departure Control advised N151U that he "appeared to be returning to Buffalo." But the pilot knew this was not the case. He told Buffalo Departure he was headed for Cleveland.

But something was wrong with the Beech C-45H. The engines were not running properly.

In the clouds and cold air where he was, the pilot assumed that ice was building in his carburetors and closing off the fuel/air mixture to the engines. He applied carburetor heat on both engines, but nothing happened. The problem persisted. Carburetor heat is a simple mechanism, similar to an automobile air vent that is opened and closed by a cable. Failure of the separate carburetor-heat controls simultaneously on both engines defies probability. But then the pilot noticed something even more improbable. Both navigation radios, which are separate from the carburetor heat and from each other, were suddenly inoperative.

"One Five One Uniform, we're having a little trouble

85

here, ah, icing up and, ah, can't get any carburetor heat. Both omni's [the two navigation radios] are off," he reported. How both navigation radios could fail while N151U was communicating with Buffalo Departure and while Buffalo Radar was still painting a target for the aircraft, is inexplicable.

N151U later disappeared from radar and attempts at communication failed. Search and rescue units were sent immediately to pick up the pieces from the presumed crash. They were directed to the spot by controllers at Buffalo Radar Departure Control. There were no pieces.

Lake Erie was combed with "no evidence" that N151U had ever existed.

The Civil Aeronautics Board studied this 1963 case thoroughly. None of the unlikely events verified in their report could be explained.

The *William B. Davoc*[3] similarly disappeared without a trace on November 11, 1940. No one knows for sure what happened to the *William B. Davoc* except that she left Erie, Pa., on November 7, 1940, loaded with coal for South Chicago; she had good radios; she passed into Lake Michigan at noon on November 10. Presumably she sank after a collision with the *Anna C. Minch*,[4] a 2880-ton steamer also lost on November 11 in Lake Michigan. Where the *William B. Davoc* sank no one knows. Half of the *Anna C. Minch* was found. She had been evenly divided. Through a process of elimination, investigators concluded that the *William B. Davoc* must have been the other ship in the collision. The *Davoc*, however, has never been found. No one survived from either ship. It is doubtful that anyone will ever know why she did not radio her plight to the outside world.

James Charles Young of Detroit was an airline transport pilot with more than 3000 hours' experience—1200 hours in Beech D-18s like the one he was flying on July 27, 1970. Young and his copilot, Carl Edwin Powell of Troy, Mich., had taken off from Rockford, Ill., about an hour about midnight on July 26. Young was a professional pilot and this was a regular run for him as well as for the Beech D-18, registration N332R.[5] They were headed home to Detroit. The weather was good. About 40 miles from Detroit and well to the south of its course, N332R was seen by several people who lived there flying back and forth over Devil's Lake in southeastern Michigan. N332R crashed into the lake. Young and Powell died. Subsequent examination of the wreckage revealed that nothing was wrong with the airplane prior to impact. No one near Devil's Lake knew either Young or Powell, according to the accident investigators. Why were they skimming the treetops as the witnesses at Devil's Lake reported? They must have been lost. But how? Why? N332R had good radios and both pilots knew the route. No doubt Young had the frequencies and courses memorized from experience. If he was having trouble, why didn't he communicate that to Air Traffic Control? The National Transportation Safety Board studied the case thoroughly. From 1970 until today, the questions have remained unanswered.

On March 31, 1950, pilot K. E. Bjorkman tried to fly from Buffalo, N.Y., to Detroit, Mich., in a Fairchild M62A-3, registration CF-FXC.[6] He left just before midnight. At 7:00 A.M., a resident of a beach cottage north of Port Huron saw the tail section of CF-FXC sticking out of the water about 1000 feet from shore in Lake Huron. That was 55 miles north of Bjorkman's intended course. Later Bjorkman was found dead in the shallow water of an adjacent beach. Canadian authorities concluded the following:

> While it is not possible to determine the cause of the accident, it is considered likely that the pilot became lost and realized that he was in danger of running out of fuel and as a result attempted to carry out a precautionary landing which resulted in his death by drowning.

Why was Bjorkman lost? Subsequent examination of his navigation radios showed no preimpact failure.

Dr. Hynek explains that such effects on radio reception are consistent with UFO proximity.

One remarkable reported physical effect [common characteristic of one type of UFO sighting] involves interference in electrical circuits causing car engines to cease functioning temporarily, radios to cut out or to exhibit uncommon static, car headlights to dim or be extinguished for a short while and, on occasion, car batteries to overheat and deteriorate rapidly.[7]

That reported effects of UFOs are consistent with so many of the unexplained Great Lakes tragedies does *not* necessarily imply any relationship between the two. However, the interference with electrical circuits is not only consistent with accidents in this chapter, but also with another group of even more curious accidents described in the following chapter.

Chapter Eight:

EFFECT ON GYROSCOPIC INSTRUMENTS

A pilot flying through the clouds has no visual reference outside the cockpit, and no human can ever control an airplane solely by his sense of equilibrium. Consequently, gyroscopic instruments are necessary for flight through clouds. In fact, pilots do not say "in the clouds." They say "on instruments." Near the Great Lakes, though, something sometimes affects normal use of instruments. No one knows what or why or how. It is known, however, that the results are often tragic.

A Cessna 182 Skylane is one of the simplest, sturdiest and easiest-to-fly of all powered aircraft in the world. An average private pilot can learn to fly it in less than an hour. Pilots say it is "gentle."

Joseph Patrick Kavanaugh, 47, had over 50 hours in Skylanes like N5271E,[1] the one he was flying on August 24, 1972. Even if he had not had that much time in Skylanes, the gentle airplane would not have offered much technical challenge to Kavanaugh. He was an airline transport pilot qualified to command a Boeing 707. Rudolph Willard Heinig, 50, was Kavanaugh's friend and fellow professional airline pilot. It was Heinig's Skylane that the two were flying that day. One person easily could have flown N5271E, but as it happened, Heinig sat in the copilot's seat while Kavanaugh sat in the pilot's seat. Kavanaugh also signed the flight plan as pilot in command. The plan was to leave Circle Pines, Minn., south of Lake Superior, at about 10:25 A.M. and head north along airway Victor 13 past Duluth to Eveleth, Minn., north of the lake.

They accepted their clearance right on time and took off at 10:33 A.M. It was a calm day. The clouds low over the airport drifted by at about four miles per hour. The low ceiling meant that Kavanaugh and Heinig would have to make the trip on instruments. This was no problem for men of their experience. As N5271E climbed into the clouds 600 feet above the runway, one of the pilots contacted Air Traffic Control, and controller Donald L. Hatterman acknowledged contact. N5271E reported as follows:

Five Two Seven One Echo off Rice Lake at 33 [minutes past the current hour] climbing to 3000 feet. Estimating Minneapolis VOR [Very-high-frequency Omni-directional Range] at 42 [minutes past that hour]. Grantsburg [will be the] next checkpoint.

Three minutes after receiving that report, Hatterman told Kavanaugh and Heinig they did not need to continue westbound out of their way to Minneapolis. Since N5271E was on radar, it was given permission to turn north to intercept the airway to Grantsburg.

N5271E never made it to Grantsburg.

The flight ended prematurely at about 10:47 A.M. August 24, 1972, in a wooded area near Anoka, Minn.

Both Kavanaugh and Heinig sustained fatal injuries.

Investigators soon determined that on impact the airplane was intact, the controls were working properly, and all instruments were impact-frozen with correct indications. What altered Kavanaugh's simple plan to fly to Eveleth?

There were two clues. Unfortunately, both led nowhere. The first was revealed by the taped conversation between Air Traffic Control and N5271E. After N5271E was turned to a northerly heading toward Lake Superior, it began having some trouble. To an aircraft, direction is measured angularly in degrees, clockwise from north. For instance, north is either 000 or 360 degrees. East is 090 degrees. South is 180, and west is 270. N5271E was supposed to be heading 360 when controller Hatterman noticed something odd.

"Cessna Five Two Seven One Echo, what is your heading now?" he asked.

"Five Two Seven One Echo shows 300 degrees turning to three six zero," answered one of the pilots.

"Okay," Hatterman acknowledged, paused, then asked, "You okay?"

N5271E answered, "Affirmative, we were having a little problem with the horizon [this is the artificial horizon, an instrument that shows how the airplane is positioned in relation to the actual horizon by displaying a tiny airplane in front of a white horizon line that moves when the airplane changes pitch or bank] but it appears to be okay now."

It is not possible to know whether Hatterman was annoyed or concerned. He answered briefly, "Okay." Then he began controlling other traffic. Two minutes later, Hatterman asked, "Cessna Seven One Echo, are you making another circle?"

This must have puzzled Kavanaugh. "What do you show for our heading now?" he asked the radar controller.

"I show you in a right turn going through west heading now almost north," the controller answered.

N5271E did not answer.

A few seconds later, Hatterman, in the Minneapolis Departure slot, said, "Seven One Echo, looks like you are in a continuous circle to the right."

Still no answer.

Twenty seconds later, Hatterman began the series of eerie transmissions that always cause a strange feeling in the heart of every pilot on the network:

Cessna Five Two Seven One Echo, Minneapolis Departure. Do you read? [pause]

Cessna Five Two Seven One Echo. Cessna Five Two Seven One Echo. Minneapolis Departure radar, do you read? [pause]

Cessna Five Two Seven One Echo. Cessna Five Two Seven One Echo. Minneapolis Departure Control. Do you read? [pause]

Cessna Five Two Seven One Echo, Five Two Seven One Echo, Minneapolis Departure Control. How do you read? [pause]

Could the airplane have suffered a failure of its gyro instruments as Kavanaugh had indicated before his sudden death? If the gyros had failed it could have caused precisely the kind of accident that killed the two. But N5271E had three gyroscopic instruments, driven by two independent power systems. No failure of one system could lead to failure of another, and two of the instruments, the artificial horizon and the turn-and-bank indicator, were electrically driven. Investigators knew the electrical system was working because the radios were working. Even if two of the three instruments had failed, either pilot was qualified to fly the airplane with any one of the surviving gyro instruments.

Another important clue turned up when scientist Ernest G. Veldey examined the instruments. Veldey confirmed that all three gyros were spinning on impact. The sudden deceleration on impact had scoured the rotors. They would not have been scoured if they had not been spinning. But there was something extraordinary about one particular gyro, the turn-and-bank. The turn-and-bank (also called turn indicator or turn coordinator) shows the pilot how fast and in which direction (right or left) he is turning. The rotor on this instrument had operated backward at one time in the instrument's life. Veldey knew this by the way the tiny carbon particles from the brushes had been flung. When a turn-and-bank rotor spins backward it causes the instrument to read precisely the *opposite* of what it should say. In other words a turn to the left shows as a turn to the right and vice versa. Anyone trying to follow it would be doomed.

This presented an obvious solution to the mystery. Kavanaugh must have noticed a discrepancy between the artificial horizon and the turn-and-bank. Since the turn-and-bank is a more reliable instrument, Veldey erroneously judged something wrong with the artificial horizon. Trying to follow the turn-and-bank would have led to precisely what happened.

But there was a serious flaw in this explanation. Veldey knew that the only thing that could cause the turn-and-bank to spin backward was for the electric current running through it to be reversed. Since the airplane current cannot switch directions by itself, Veldey assumed that the wires connected to the back of the turn-and-bank had been reversed. Veldey examined the wires attached to the back of the instrument, and he examined the broken wires in the instrument panel that had been torn from the instrument.

The turn-and-bank in N5271E was wired properly. Investigators had to conclude that the turn-and-bank had been wired improperly at some previous time in its life, and that the problem had been corrected before the flight that ended August 24, 1972. To suggest anything else would be outrageous.

Consequently, the probable cause of the accident that destroyed N5271E and killed Kavanaugh and Heinig remains "undetermined."

Eight years before, a Piper PA-22, N3142Z,[2] under command of a 40-year-old commercial pilot, was on top of an overcast in northern Illinois. At 3:47 P.M., December 23, 1964, the pilot contacted Flight Service, a government program to provide pilots with information pertinent to flight operations. He told Flight Service his directional gyro had tumbled and was unusable. This is a curious report in itself, since mere tumbling of a directional gyro is a self-correcting problem if the pilot can keep the airplane under control for a couple of minutes. But N3142Z wanted to know where there were breaks in the overcast so that the flight could descend visually without penetrating the clouds.

Flight Service told N3142Z to stand by while the briefer checked nearby weather observations. About ten seconds later, the briefer tried to call the pilot to answer the pilot's question. No contact was made. Flight Service must have assumed that if the pilot had needed the information, he would have called back. Two days later authorities learned the pilot was missing. A search quickly found the wreckage. Examination showed "there was no evidence of any preimpact malfunction or failure of the aircraft; and no physical evidence was found to indicate the aircraft gyros were not capable of normal operation." Since the pilot should have known more about the weather before he took off, "inadequate flight preparation" was listed as one of the probable causes. The others were "a loss of control for undetermined reasons" and "loss of directional gyro function for an undisclosed reason."

You may recall it was a gyro failure that accompanied the strange fires and seasickness that plagued the Coast Guard ships searching for the tanker barge *Clevco*,[3] which disappeared so many times on December 2, 1942. That directional gyro, like the turn-and-bank on board N5271E, was electric.

It is important to note that the examples cited here are taken from accident files. Through more than 90 percent of all flights and lake shipping, a gyro failure has no serious effect on safety. And even during the few crucial times when a gyro failure would make flight more difficult, only a total loss of all gyro instruments or a confusing malfunction can make control impossible. There is no way to know how many thousands of gyro instruments have failed, then cured themselves for no apparent reason over the Great Lakes. Only a small fraction would ever become accidents and show up in the public files some of which are sources for this chapter.

A Lear 23 is a small, sleek corporate jet. Lear N804LJ[4] was being operated by its manufacturer, Lear Jet Corporation of Wichita, Kans., on October 21, 1965. That was the day it was used to deliver a Lear Jet official to Detroit at 5:40 P.M. The pilot in command was Glen E. David, 32, a commercial pilot with over 2000 hours in jets, more than 600 in Lears. The copilot was Lawrence V. Bangiola, a commercial instructor pilot with more than 8000 hours' experience.

Just before 7:00 P.M. on October 21, N804LJ was sitting on the ramp at Detroit Airport waiting to go back to Wichita when Detroit Clearance Delivery transmitted N804LJ's clearance. Because of some traffic problems on the taxiways, it was almost a half-hour before N804LJ took off. Four minutes later N804LJ contacted Cleveland Center, and reported passing through flight level 180 (approximately 18,000 feet) on the way to the assigned altitude, flight level 250.

But peculiar things began happening to Lear N804LJ. The Cleveland Center sector controller who handled Detroit Sector started to hand off N804LJ to the adjacent sector to the west. N804LJ was headed away from Lake Erie toward Lake Michigan. N804LJ acknowledged the instructions to contact the new controller on a new frequency. Inside Cleveland Center the first controller pointed out N804LJ's target on the radar display and told the second controller to expect contact. Changing frequency takes about as long as changing channels on a television set. But N804LJ did not call the new controller. Instead the jet sped silently westward through the sector. The controller that N804LJ was supposed to call later recalled the incident:

(N804LJ) . . . was handed off to me by the Jackson Departure radar controller at approximately 7:33 P.M. The aircraft at that time was approximately 25 nautical miles east-northeast of the Jackson, Mich., VOR radio fix and heading approximately 250 degrees west-south-west.

I placed a radar marker on the aircraft target and followed it for about 10 miles to the southwest when the aircraft started a sharp turn to the right. As the aircraft passed through a northerly heading the beacon target disappeared from the radar. I immediately turned up the normal radar gain, but never saw the aircraft on radar again.

Center controllers live in a complicated electronic world where a strange technical language is jabbered. Controllers do not lack feeling or sensitivity for those whose lives they control, but such sentiment is of little use in their abstract, three-dimensional, real-time game of preventing dots from merging. The Cleveland Center controller awaiting handoff of N804LJ notified his superiors of the target's disappearance and continued at his display station until he could be relieved to begin writing the reports.

To witnesses near where the flight ended unexpectedly, the display was much less abstract, much more spectacular. They "generally described seeing a large ball of fire followed by many burning parts falling in an umbrella or fan-shaped pattern."

Pilots David and Bangiola were killed on impact. The accident was not survivable. In fact, it took some of the Army's and the FBI's best scientists to determine that there were two people aboard. (The U.S. Army's battlefield identification experts are renowned through the world among accident investigators for their technical expertise.)

On March 2, 1966, after a five-month investigation of the crash, a public hearing was held at Lassen Motor Hotel, Wichita, Kans. Dozens of government and Lear Jet scientists as well as journalists converged to study the evidence. Unfortunately the evidence raised more questions than the experts could answer.

Eleven days after the beginning of the public hearing, CAB group chairman Robert Rudich secretly recommended the following conclusions:

1. The crew encountered an in-flight emergency situation with which they were unable to cope and still maintain altitude or directional control of the aircraft.
2. The nature and extent of the emergency are not known.

But the aviation public needed a more specific answer than the one Rudich proposed. Dozens of experts worked feverishly with no resolution in sight. FBI and Army pathologists examined every fragment of human tissue and clothing. Engineers and metallurgists studied every fragment of the wreckage right down to the chemical analysis of insulation on the electrical wiring. The Air Traffic Control experts reenacted the flight over and over again for clues about what might have happened aboard N804LJ. Human-factor investigators interviewed everyone even remotely connected with the crew—relatives, employers, past employers, lovers and even lovers'

lovers. Government scientists along with the Lear Jet Corporation's best engineers spent countless hours studying the aircraft—every structure, every system, every modification or even possible modification that N804LJ had gone through. The corporation's chief executive officer, Bill Lear, became personally involved in the search for an answer. But their efforts were frustrated. One example of this frustration came when Human Factors Group Chairman John J. Carroll submitted one classified secret report on what his group had accomplished.

The document was typed, single-spaced. It was a cursory explanation of the evidence gathered. Still it was 18 pages long. Its conclusion, simple and brief, in its entirety reads as follows:

> Based upon this evidence, it is concluded that two persons, Glen David and Lawrence V. Bangiola, were aboard N804LJ, and perished in the accident near Jackson, Mich., on October 21, 1965.
>
> There is no evidence to support possible inflight incapacitation of either or both crew members; there is no evidence of foul play.

Ultimately the investigation centered on N804LJ's electric gyro system. The impact-frozen instrument readings were not consistent with one another. Something had to have gone wrong. The radio magnetic indicator, this airplane's primary directional gyroscope, displayed a 360-degree heading (due north) on impact. "The heading conforms to neither the 260-degree heading [west] of the other instruments, nor the 335-degree heading [northwest] at impact," says the final public report. N804LJ's atitude indicator was similarly affected.

Although the experts were not unanimous on the point, it was decided that the gyroscopic instrument failures might have made the jet uncontrollable that night in what may have been moderate turbulence above the clouds. Even those who disagreed had no better alternative explanation.

Something fouled the dual alternating-current electrical systems in N804LJ—one right after the other was destroyed. This left David and Bangiola unable to control the westbound aircraft.

After more than two years, the National Transportation Safety Board, on December 11, 1967, adopted its report for what turned out to be one of the most thoroughly investigated general aviation accidents in the history of the world. The report details many things about what must have happened in the airspace between Lake Erie and Lake Michigan the night of October 21, 1965. The conclusion: There is no explanation for what destroyed both electrical systems. There is no explanation for David and Bangiola's failure to report their plight to Air Traffic Control.

Chapter Nine:

VARIOUS THEORIES

In *The Bermuda Triangle*, Charles Berlitz puts forth a collection of bizarre theories to explain the well-documented concentration of peculiar tragedies that have struck that part of the Atlantic Ocean. Some are repeated here because of their remarkable applicability to strikingly similar phenomena recorded in the Great Lakes.

One such theory Berlitz reports is that of electrical engineer and author Hugh Auchincloss Brown, who says:

> There are good reasons to connect these incidents to the magnetic field of the earth. There have been fearful reverses of the magnetic field at different periods of the earth's history and perhaps another age of a change in the magnetic situation is developing, with occasional magnetic "earthquake" indications as prior warnings.[1]

Berlitz believes this could cause airplanes to disappear. And indeed, airplanes, especially when flying in the clouds, are very much dependent on accurate and consistent readings of the earth's magnetic field. Consequently, aeronautic charts of the Great Lakes contain a number of warnings about the strange locations where these anomalies have been thoroughly verified. If such attacks occur during instrument flight when they are not anticipated, they could cause serious problems for the flight crew. Some of the reported gyro failures could actually have been compass malfunctions. Pilots who could not reconcile their gyros with their compass might very likely have interpreted the problem as gyro failure.

The Great Lakes display a variety of magnetic peculiarities besides the famous mysteries of eastern Lake Ontario. The entire western Great Lakes region is underlain by rich iron deposits. In fact, it is the center of the U.S. iron-mining, iron-transporting and iron-processing industries.

Perhaps the most famous of the theories put forth by Dr. Berlitz is the line of zero magnetic deviation. Magnetic north, the direction a compass points, is rarely the same as true north, the direction toward the north pole. The difference between true north and magnetic north is "magnetic variation." For example, the magnetic variation at Henryetta, Okla., is about eight degrees easterly. This means that a compass needle will point eight degrees to the east of true north. If one wanted to follow a compass true north, he should follow a heading of 352 degrees—or eight degrees left of the compass indication north. Such information is relayed to navigators by "isogonic lines" on navigational charts. These lines connect points of equal magnetic variation. There is one such line, the "agonic line," that runs through the Great Lakes southward, curving more southeastward toward the Atlantic, where it crosses the southern part of the Bermuda Triangle.

Berlitz calls this line by its description—the line of zero magnetic variation. Points along this line are where a compass needle points to true north, where magnetic north and true north are the same direction. In theory and in practice navigation in the vicinity of this line is simpler. Yet, for some reason, statistics show a large concentration of most peculiar tragedies along this line— the *Bannockburn,* Northwest Airlines Flight 2501, the *Alpena,* the *Kamloops,* the *Cerisolles,* the *Bautzen,* the *D. M. Clemson,* United Airlines Flight 389, the *Benjamin Noble,* N212AD, N1021B, and the *Rouse Simmons,* to name a few.

Berlitz is not specific on how this line could relate to such events, but he has suggested certain possibilities. One is that the arrivals and departures of interplanetary travelers might create problems for ships and airplanes. Berlitz' suggestion is that for reasons of their own, these aliens choose to enter and leave planet Earth along the agonic line.

Berlitz also suggests the possibility of "space kidnappings."[2] If one accepts the notion of "spacemen," then motivation for such activity is easily understood by considering what Earth scientists could do if they were abroad under the same circumstances. And if the alien scientists are entering and leaving planet Earth along the agonic line, then both the Great Lakes and the Bermuda Triangle would be ideal places for these foreign scientists to isolate and gather specimens for their research. One incident remarkably consistent with this theory of intentional intervention was the Walesville, N.Y., case and the Keeweenau Point UFO (both discussed in Chapter Three).

Another theory put forth by Berlitz is that of Ivan Sanderson, who suggests the presence of "vortices in and out of which material objects can drop into or out of other space-time continua."[3] While such explanations may seem farfetched, they do mesh with the extraordinary number of equally farfetched cases over and on the Great Lakes in which ground stations have continued radio conversations with ships and aircraft that have long since disappeared on radar and to the naked eye.

Two cases in particular seem so incredible that nothing short of such a theory could explain them. One is the case of N999NJ. The other is what happened to N8071Y.

It was in 1950 that the Navy turned its sophisticated sonar equipment to the bottom of Lake Michigan in search of missing Northwest Airlines Flight 2501. They never found the airliner, but the authorities presumed that it crashed about 20 miles west of the east shore of Lake Michigan, somewhere between Benton Harbor, Mich., and South Haven, Mich. The "Victor Airways" that now crisscross the country were just being established then. A few years after the disappearance of Northwest Flight 2501, no one noticed or cared that three new Victor Airways traversed the area where Northwest 2501 was thought to have vanished. They were Victor 100, Victor 193 and Victor 116. Some 18 years after Northwest 2501, in 1968, a most curious event occurred on

Victor 116, just about 20 miles from the east shore of Lake Michigan.

James Edmund Looker was then 50. He was a professional pilot who had been flying since he was 18. He had once worked for the Federal Aviation Administration. Later he became a test pilot for Piper Aircraft. Later still he worked as a charter pilot for Wellsville (N.Y.) Flying Service. In 1966 he took a job as pilot for S.C.M. Corporation, where his only duty was to fly board chairman Dr. E. H. Litchfield. As of March 8, 1968, he had 10,000 hours' experience. The Litchfield airplane was a large DeHavilland Dove, registration number N999NJ.[4] It was well equipped with avionics—a sophisticated autopilot that could fly N999NJ right down to its destination runway, and weather radar that could search miles ahead for potential problems.

On this March 8, Looker and Dr. Litchfield and Mrs. Litchfield left LaGuardia Airport, New York City, to return to their homebase, Wellsville, N.Y. There they picked up Litchfield's mother and two children, filled up the tanks with fuel and departed for Chicago's Meigs Field at 6:00 P.M. Just before 8:00 P.M. N999NJ contacted Cleveland Center. At 8:30 P.M. Cleveland Center handed off the flight to Chicago Center, and N999NJ picked up an hour because of the time difference. Shortly after 7:30 P.M., N999NJ told Chicago Center it was in excellent weather with more than 12 miles' visibility. It was on Airway Victor 116 approaching Lake Michigan.

Then at 7:50 P.M. the first of many rather odd transmissions came from N999NJ. Looker said, ". . . we indicate about one seven five to one eight zero. Ground speed now one four five." This meant that N999NJ was making a true airspeed of more than 190 knots (220 miles per hour), but he was only flying 145 knots (167 miles per hour) ground speed. If this was correct, N999NJ was suffering what would amount to a 45- or 50-knot (52 or 58 miles per hour) headwind. The reason this was odd is that there was only a mild breeze on the surface—and that would have been a *tailwind* to N999NJ. Balloons used to measure the winds aloft in that area didn't show anything consistent with N999NJ's report.

N999NJ was 20 miles from the east shore of Lake Michigan, 20 miles east of Benton Harbor, when the next curious event occurred.

According to the controller at Chicago Center, N999NJ vanished from radar.

The controller advised N999NJ that radar contact was lost.

N999NJ gave the controller his altitude and position.

Still the controller could not paint an echo from N999NJ, nor could he get a reply from N999NJ's transponder. The transponder should have been transmitting automatically a coded response every time it was interrogated by Chicago Center radar. Any failure of the transponder to reply should have been immediately apparent to Looker. But Looker was at a loss to explain his invisible condition.

Twelve minutes later, at 8:18 P.M., N999NJ contacted Meigs Tower, reported good weather and asked for clearance into the airport. Since N999NJ was still invisible to radar, the Meigs tower controller told him to report when he crossed "Surf," a radio-navigation fix on Lake Michigan just a few miles east of Meigs.

Two minutes later, at 8:20 P.M., N999NJ reported at Surf. Looker was now within power-off gliding distance of land.

N999NJ was still invisible to Chicago radar.

Through Looker's report, Meigs Tower knew where he was. So, even though the airplane could not be seen visually or on radar from the tower, it was given a clearance into the control zone.

That was 8:20 P.M. on March 8.

N999NJ did not acknowledge.

Meigs Tower tried several more times to make contact.

An extensive search of Lake Michigan turned up all but one of the bodies. The DeHavilland Dove, however, remains in a yet unknown location. The accident report describes how thoroughly—and unsuccessfully—the searchers combed Lake Michigan:

A search has been conducted by the U.S. Coast Guard and two private agencies of the area of the aircraft's

103

last reported position. The U.S. Coast Guard conducted visual surface and dragging operations and the two private agencies conducted sonar searches of the area with negative results.

Why couldn't N999NJ be found?

Why didn't anyone in Chicago see a large aircraft crash just off shore?

Why couldn't Chicago Center radar pick up N999NJ or its transponder?

Why didn't Looker transmit a distress call?

Why did N999NJ crash?

How could the bodies have been discovered with no evidence of airplane wreckage?

Some of the world's foremost authorities in accident investigation have studied these questions. They have no answers.

On December 6, 1967, four days before Otis Redding's mysterious death, Lee Norman Sanborn, a 45-year-old professional pilot from Grand Rapids, Mich., began what was to become one of the most bizarre flights in U.S. civil aviation history. The flight was a commercial air taxi flight, a return from Cleveland, Ohio, where Sanborn had dropped off three passengers. Sanborn worked for Northern Air Service, Inc. The airplane was a multi-engine Piper PA-30, registration number N8071Y[5] Sanborn was an experienced instrument pilot. Within the preceding 90 days he had flown more than 40 hours in actual instrument conditions. He'd flown four hours on instruments within the 24 hours preceding this flight.

The curious events surrounding this flight began as N8071Y returned to its homebase, Grand Rapids, Mich. The flight was preparing for an Instrument Landing System approach to runway 26 at the Grand Rapids Airport. It was an approach with which Sanborn was intimately familiar.

From the Lansing, Mich., radio fix to the Odessa fix is 18 miles. N8071Y was proceeding west-northwest along this airway when he was handed off to Grand Rapids Approach Control at 6:02 P.M. At that time he told Grand Rapids that he was estimating that he would cross the final approach fix at 6:07 P.M. He asked about the weather on the surface. It was drizzling, but visibility was almost a mile. Sanborn laughed and asked the weather observers to keep the weather like that until he got there. He knew he would not have to miss the approach unless it got worse.

The final approach fix was on the Instrument Landing System course about five miles from the runway threshold. It was, and is still, called the outer marker. Approach controller Richard L. Hoppe cleared N8071Y to proceed to the final approach fix and begin a holding pattern there at 4000 feet. The 4000-foot altitude assignment would allow a United Airlines Viscount ahead of N8071Y to make its approach passing beneath N8071Y. Immediately after N8071Y had reported level at 4000 feet, Grand Rapids Approach transmitted, "Seven One Yankee, if you can start slowing it up just a little bit now we should be able to work you straight in. The Viscount should be at the marker [the final approach fix directly under N8071Y] very shortly."

"Okay, will do," Sanborn said as he began reducing airspeed in preparation for the approach.

Approach controller Hoppe asked, "Okay, you are well established on the localizer [the final approach course that made up one leg of the holding pattern] now?"

"That's affirm," said Sanborn.

It is difficult to cite examples, but Sanborn's relaxed tone and his ability to volunteer unsolicited position reports when he saw that it would expedite other traffic show that he was not only alert but familiar with the approach and conscious of where the rest of the traffic was. These facts make subsequent events even more unbelievable.

At 6:10 P.M. controller Hoppe cleared Sanborn to descend from 4000 and begin the approach, but he instructed Sanborn not to cross the final approach fix until 6:12 P.M. It was necessary under the system then in effect that aircraft be at least two minutes apart on the final approach course. All were in the clouds and unable to see each other. Hoppe transmitted a current time check to Sanborn.

But Sanborn arrived at the final approach fix a few seconds early. It was a common kind of mistake. Sanborn may have underestimated the speed he would pick up descending to the final approach altitude, 2500 feet.

To maintain proper separation, the tower controller, Kenneth J. Poirier, instructed Sanborn to make a 360-degree turn—a complete circle—to the right. This would take two minutes and put N8071Y right back on the final approach course at the outer marker. Sanborn was told to report back when he had completed the circle. Sanborn was also told that he was only 30 seconds early at the final approach fix.

Two minutes later, at 6:13 P.M., as expected, Sanborn reported that he had completed the circle and was back at the final approach fix headed inbound toward the airport.

Poirier cleared Sanborn to land. The United Airlines Viscount was already safely turning off the runway.

Sanborn acknowledged the clearance to proceed inbound and land.

Since Sanborn was on his way from the final approach fix to the runway, Approach Control cleared another airline flight, Miller 81, a Cessna 402, to make the approach, but told Miller 81 not to pass the final approach fix until 6:15 P.M., once again to ensure the two-minute separation.

Miller 81 hit the final approach fix right on time—6:15 P.M.—and he was cleared to land.

It takes about two or three minutes to get from the final approach fix to the runway threshold, and at 6:15 P.M. tower controller Poirier was expecting to see N8071Y break out of the clouds. If N8071Y didn't break out then, it would mean that Miller 81 behind him would be getting too close. Poirier transmitted a question to Sanborn. "Seven One Yankee, do you have [visual contact with] the approach lights yet?"

Then Sanborn said something very curious and very frightening.

"Negative, sir, we're just coming up on the marker now." Ordinarily this would have meant that N8071Y had reached the final approach fix, known as the outer marker.

But no one in the control tower could believe that. It had been more than three minutes since Sanborn had reported passing that fix inbound. "Seven One Yankee, you coming up on the middle marker?" Poirier asked, referring to an insignificant radio fix about half a mile from the threshold.

Sanborn said, "Negative, on the outer marker," five miles away.

This was impossible. Where could N8071Y have been for the previous three minutes? Sanborn had said he was at the final approach fix three minutes before. He must have heard the tower clear Miller 81 to land. He must have known that Miller 81 was two minutes behind him. Yet all of a sudden Miller 81 was at least a minute ahead of N8071Y and N8071Y did not know it. N8071Y was still making the 360-degree turn that he had already reported completing—a turn he had been instructed to make more than five minutes before.

Incredibly, Sanborn was not alarmed. He was only puzzled. "You gave us a [emphasis added] 360 back to the marker," he said.

The tower couldn't believe it. "Seven One Yankee, you said you were at the *outer* marker—is that correct?" said Poirier, who was still trying to gather his wits.

Sanborn replied, "Negative, we're not at the outer marker. You gave us a 360 back to the marker." Pilot Sanborn still didn't understand. He was totally oblivious to everything that had happened within the previous minutes. As far as he was concerned he had arrived at the final approach fix a few seconds earlier. He had been instructed to make a 360-degree turn to the right. Now, all of a sudden people in the tower were asking if he could see the approach lights more than five miles away. He wasn't even back around to the final approach fix yet.

Hoppe started to warn Miller 81. "Miller 81, Miller 81, you on?" he asked. This was his way of asking Miller 81 if he was listening and knew what was happening.

But there was no time to wait for a reply. A collision was imminent. Another plane, North Central Airlines

Flight 346, was now headed down toward N8071Y. Poirier, trying to remain calm, transmitted a new clearance to N8071Y. "Okay, Seven One Yankee, climb and maintain 3500 and cancel your approach clearance," he said. Then Hoppe told the airliner above Sanborn, "North Central 346, climb to and maintain 4500." This would get North Central 346 out of Sanborn's way.

Sanborn acknowledged the new clearance. So did North Central 346. At 6:18 P.M., N8071Y reported reaching 3500.

At the same time Miller 81 reported seeing the airport lights, so the final approach course was completely clear. The approach controller cleared Sanborn once again for the approach. He told Sanborn to report crossing the outer marker.

A few minutes later North Central 346, which was still holding, waiting for his own approach clearance, called Approach Control and asked, "It's taking a long time for that approach, isn't it?"

With that, Grand Rapids Tower asked, "Seven One Yankee, have you reached the marker inbound yet?"

Sanborn didn't answer.

Dawn Dietz, a 12-year-old girl playing in her front year near Lowell, Mich., was the last person to actually see N8071Y. The investigation report says:

At 6:10 P.M. an airplane flew over her house going north to south. The airplane was so low she was frightened and thought it was going to hit her garage. She remembered seeing the red and green lights on the wingtips. She was so frightened she took her sister and ran into the house, locked the front door and ran into a bedroom. After she was in the bedroom she heard a crash. When her mother and father arrived home at approximately 6:35 P.M. she informed them of the indent and after some discussion her father called the Kent County Airport. The father, Mr. Dietz, then stated he and neighbors started a search of the area.

They found N8071Y. Sanborn was dead. The airplane clock was still running. Miss Dietz' recollection of the time of impact, 6:10 P.M., was dismissed even though she recalled so many other details accurately. At 6:10 P.M.

Sanborn was just acknowledging his first clearance. But the four controllers who followed the sequence of events surrounding the more than three-minute disappearance of N8071Y could not be ignored. Everything they said or heard was still on tape. A transcript of that tape is still held by the National Archives in Washington.

The accident itself produced some startling mysteries. First, all the aircraft systems including the instruments and radios functioned normally when tested after the crash. The Federal Aviation Administration checked all the radio navigation aids on the ground. All were working normally. Sanborn had just passed his six-month flight check for instrument competency the previous week. The stringent six-month checks are required only of commercial pilots flying passengers and cargo for hire through bad weather. Sanborn had proved his ability to cope with the most unusual emergencies.

Another mystery was the way the controls were set. Sanborn had the throttles all the way back to the idle position on both engines. He had the gear and wing-flap controls in the down position. Everything was set up as though he were getting ready to touch down on the airport's runway. Instead he was seven miles from the airport crashing through trees in the middle of a swamp. The controls were not set the way they should have been in preparation for a crash landing. In fact, the autopilot was flying the airplane.

The last question is almost as puzzling as the missing three minutes. If Sanborn was low enough to scare the wits out of a 12-year-old girl, if he was clearly visible to her, why didn't he see where he was? Why didn't he realize his problem? Why was there no distress call?

The questions are similar to those left after the strange disappearance of Dr. Litchfield's DeHavilland Dove N999NJ.

Why are there so many of these occurrences along the agonic line?

Are there "magnetic earthquakes," "space kidnappings," or "space-time vortices" as Berlitz suggests? What is the explanation?

Chapter Ten:

THE CLOUDY SHROUD

Over the Great Lakes pilots flying "on instruments" sometimes cannot control their airplanes. The pilots are qualified. The air is smooth. The aircraft are sound.
The reason is unknown.

When a pilot learns to fly, he learns to control an airplane by looking at the horizon. With a little practice the pilot learns to fly when the horizon is hazy or indefinite by using other visual references—the ground directly below, stars, distant shorelines, points of light or even clouds if he is between layers. This is all called visual flight. But when a pilot flies into a cloud he loses visual reference. If there is no turbulence, the aircraft may keep itself upright for several minutes. If the turbulence is severe, the airplane may tumble out of control within seconds. The only way that a pilot can control the flight is by reference to his gyroscopic instruments. This takes some special training, and one of the biggest causes, if not the biggest cause, of fatal airplane accidents is untrained pilots attempting visual flight into clouds.

Sometimes this can happen at night without warning. The pilot never knows the cloud is there until he is in it. At other times it may come from avoiding a more immediate danger, like pulling up into the clouds to avoid colliding with rising terrain. Quite often the visual pilot gets stuck on top of an overcast. But circumstances notwithstanding, the underlying cause almost always is the inexperienced pilot's ignorance about how really serious this mistake is.

Learning to fly by reference to instruments is not difficult. It takes only about two hours to teach a visual pilot how to control an airplane without visual reference. In 10 to 15 hours he can be doing complex maneuvers. And in about 40 hours he can carry on a flight crosscountry and make an approach into an airport he cannot see with most of his instruments inoperative. To get the instrument rating he must prove he can do all of this while making navigation calculations, maintaining communication with Air Traffic Control and monitoring all aircraft systems. Beyond that he must pass a stringent written examination designed to test his knowledge of navigation, radios, instruments, aerodynamics and especially weather. He must prove that he can recover from any number of unusual critical positions using only the instruments.

I've given instrument instruction to many pilots. A few were so nervous I doubted their ability to make decisions under pressure. Others were so calm I doubted their judgment. But I've never flown with a current instrument pilot who has caused me to doubt his ability to at least keep the airplane under control. Nevertheless, accident files from the Great Lakes are filled with disasters where qualified, and often highly experienced, instrument pilots have *completely* lost control of their airplanes for no apparent reason.

Dennis Head was an instrument-rated flight instructor— a professional pilot who flew every day. He was 23 years old when he died on November 10, 1969, in Chicago.

Head had taken off in a Piper PA-32, N3262W,[1] from DuPage Airport in Chicago and was headed for Midway Airport 28 miles away. The weather was not bad, but it was bad enough that Instrument Flight Rules were safer than visual flight. Approach Control at Midway directed Head toward the localizer course, a kind of radio beam that leads a pilot directly to the threshold of the runway. Head was given radar vectors to join the localizer and cleared for the approach. But instead of joining the localizer, Head flew right through it.

Something was wrong. Midway Approach advised N3262W of its position and gave it a vector that would point it back toward the localizer. The PA-32 disappeared from radar. It had crashed in a Chicago alley.

The cause of the accident was labeled "spatial disorientation."

Why did a professional pilot who had flown through that area hundreds of times, often in worse weather, just simply and suddenly lose control of his aircraft? No one knows. It wasn't as though he'd gotten in worse weather than he expected. It was a short flight and he knew exactly what the weather was. The ceiling was more than 200 feet above minimums and visibility was good enough that he could have flown by Visual Flight Rules if he'd wanted.

Spatial disorientation is an aeromedical term describing an inability to determine one's attitude in relation to the earth. For example, one may believe he is on his right side when really he is on his left side. An easy way to demonstrate the phenomenon is to put someone in a swivel chair, ask him to close his eyes and begin turning the chair 40 to 60 revolutions per minute, say to the right. Then ask the subject to describe his motion. At first he will tell you correctly he is turning to the right. After a minute or two, perhaps less, he will mistakenly report that he is slowing down. A short while later, he will tell you he believes he has stopped, or almost stopped. At this point, if you do stop the chair abruptly, the subject will tell you he is being violently spun to the left. When he opens his eyes, his eyeballs will shudder back and forth and he may become queasy.

None of this would happen if the subject had his eyes open. We have learned from a lifetime of experience to let our vision overrule our sense of equilibrium.

When a pilot is trained to fly on instruments, he develops reflex judgments that allow the instruments to replace the natural visual references to which he has been accustomed all his life. As long as the pilot is experienced enough that the instruments overrule his sense of equilibrium and as long as the instruments work properly, he should never become spatially disoriented.

Victor 2 is an airway that runs east and west across the United States. It runs through Syracuse, N.Y., and passes just north of downtown Detroit, Mich. N1244Z,[2] a Beechcraft 95-55, was at Detroit City Airport southwest of the city on the morning of January 12, 1963. N1244Z left the airport about noon with two passengers and an instrument-qualified pilot. The pilot had more than 4000 hours' experience. The weather was not bad, but even when it is marginal as it was on January 12, 1963, it is easier and safer for a qualified pilot to enter the clouds on Instrument Flight Rules than to confine himself to the restricted volume of clear air where Visual Flight Rules apply.

N1244Z's flight plan was filed under Instrument Flight Rules. After takeoff it climbed into the clouds headed northward to join Victor 2. Upon reaching the airway, it would turn eastward toward its destination, Syracuse. N1244Z was more than 1000 feet up into the clouds and climbing to its assigned altitude, 7000 feet, when the pilot reported joining Victor 2. The radar operator at District Metropolitan Airport, which is several miles east of Detroit City Airport, watched N1244Z turn right from its northerly course to an easterly one.

Then the unusual happened.

N1244Z disappeared from radar.

The pilot never said why, but witnesses on the ground reported that with both engines screaming, he came diving out of the clouds into the ground in what authorities described as a "near-vertical descent." The word "descent" is somewhat of an understatement in this case.

N1244Z and the three aboard penetrated three inches of solid concrete and the underlying ground to a depth of six feet six inches. For the accident investigators it was a grisly job, but one for which they were well equipped. After the meticulous and tedious task of putting the pieces back together, they came to an extraordinary conclusion, just as they have so many other times in this small region.

There was no reason for the crash.

On October 24, 1971, Dr. and Mrs. Edward S. Rambasek of Strongville, Ohio, and their friends Mr. and Mrs. Robert J. Roehm were returning to their homes near

Cleveland after a Florida holiday. They flew in their Cessna 320, N4149T,[3] according to Instrument Flight Rules from Tampa to Knoxville, where they refueled. At Knoxville, Dr. Rambasek, a qualified instrument pilot, studied the weather along his route to Cleveland Hopkins Airport, and filed his instrument flight plan.

At 4:23 P.M., N4149T was proceeding north, passing from Atlanta Center to Indianapolis Center, and finally at 6:07 P.M. it was handed off to Cleveland Center. The Cleveland Center controller that was handling N4149T cleared it down to 7000. Then the Center controller picked up his direct line to the controller at Cleveland Tower who was handling approaches. (This air traffic control position within Cleveland Tower is called Cleveland Approach.) Through this contact, Cleveland Center was able to point out N4149T's target for Cleveland Approach.

Cleveland Center then called N4149T and instructed him to contact Cleveland Approach. N4149T did not acknowledge. Cleveland Center tried again—and again. Then the controller picked up the direct line to Cleveland Approach again. Perhaps N4149T had changed frequencies as instructed without acknowledging? But Cleveland Approach had not been contacted. So, Cleveland Approach tried to initiate contact.

Still the bright target moved across the radar screen. At 6:18 P.M., N4149T disappeared from radar.

At approximately that same time, Mrs. Melvin E. Markley first noticed a big multi-engine aircraft racing downward. Her description follows:

The motors sounded like a dive bomber in a dive. Real loud, trying to pull up. It seemed to pull up level then went a ways on a side angle then it dipped. Then it exploded with a flash.

All aboard died.

Investigators combed the wreckage looking for clues. The engines were working on impact. The flight controls were intact on impact. Gyros were spinning properly on impact.

The cause of the accident was obvious—spatial disorientation.

But Rambasek was qualified. Pilots who knew him testified to this effect. They were disturbed. "Dr. Rambasek was qualified in the Cessna 320 and would not have lost control of the aircraft from lack of skill," said one.

I never knew Rambasek, but I tend to agree with those who flew with him. My reasons, however, stem from other information—the aircraft equipment list filed away with the accident report. N4149T was equipped with a sophisticated autopilot that would have allowed the world's worst instrument pilot to make a perfect letdown through the overcast.

Why did Rambasek lose control, killing himself, his wife and his friends? No explanations have been offered.

Dr. Robert A. Rufflo and his wife Beatrice, along with Jerome and Irene Pizer, all of Milwaukee, left Billy Mitchell Field, where Rufflo's plane was kept. They left shortly after noon, November 18, 1970. Rufflo was a 41-year-old surgeon and qualified instrument pilot. The airplane was a Piper PA-24-180, registration number N7880P.[4] The group was headed for Mosinee, Wisc., between Lake Superior and Lake Michigan.

It was a calm day with ceilings and visibility low enough to justify Instrument Flight Rules. One hour after takeoff from Milwaukee, Chicago Center cleared N7880P to descend from its cruising altitude of 6000 feet down to 4000 feet in preparation for its approach into Central Wisconsin Airport at Mosinee. N7880P was probably already in the clouds at 6000, but he was almost certainly without visual reference by the time he descended to 4000.

Eight minutes after the descent clearance, at 1:13 P.M., N7880P reported, "level at 4000."

Four minutes later N7880P transmitted, "Ah, Center, Eight Zero Pop, do you have, ah, most current Wausau weather and wind again?"

Chicago Center gave him the weather at Wausau, only a few miles from his destination.

N7880P acknowledged.

At 1:31 P.M., Chicago Center asked N7880P to make a position report.

"Eight Zero Pop, 2700 procedure turn," came the answer.

Aircraft making that approach in 1970 were required to fly away from the airport on a specified course at 3000 feet above sea level. After a few minutes they were to make a "procedure turn" of 180 degrees that would head them back to the airport. The approach allowed them to descend to 2700 feet after the procedure turn. N7880P's position report put him in this procedure turn.

Approximately 60 seconds after that position report, the clock in N7880P stopped. It stopped right about where one would expect N7880P to be making its procedure turn.

It was impact-frozen at 1:32 P.M.

It marked the exact time the flight ended. It marked the time of death for Dr. and Mrs. Robert A. Rufflo and Mr. and Mrs. Jerome W. Pizer.

Again the authorities went through the exercise of eliminating various causes. Finally it was clear that the accident was the result of spatial disorientation—spatial disorientation so severe Rufflo couldn't even control his airplane.

This mystery was never solved.

Investigators had a similar problem with the crash of a multi-engine Cessna 310G, N512R,[5] on May 23, 1973, at Ann Arbor, Mich., just west of Lake Erie. The pilot, who was qualified for instrument flight, took off with two passengers for a business trip to Kansas City. He took off under Instrument Flight Rules, but somehow during the departure, he lost control of the twin Cessna. The pilot and two passengers were killed in the crash. There is also no explanation for the "spatial disorientation" in this case.

Guy R. Cordell, a 36-year-old qualified instrument pilot, was a professional. And like a professional he was concerned, but not alarmed, by the deteriorating weather as he approached Iron Mountain, Wisc., on the evening of October 29, 1967. He had left Morris, Ill., without filing a flight plan for his multi-engine Beech C-45H, registration N956C.[6]

It is common in the United States for visual flights to be conducted with no flight plan. But when briefers at Joliet, Ill., Radio told Cordell to expect instrument weather farther north, he filed an instrument flight plan and told them he would pick up his clearance as he overflew Milwaukee. He did just that at 7:30 P.M. He was estimating Iron Mountain at 8:26 P.M., but Minneapolis Center put him in a holding pattern high above his destination. He flew the pattern about eight times on solid instruments until he was cleared for the approach at 9:05 P.M., a half-hour after his estimated time of arrival.

When an aircraft makes an instrument approach it descends to a certain height above the runway. It is called the "decision height." At the decision height, if the pilot sees the airport he lands. If he doesn't he climbs back up to begin the approach again. N956C did neither. Despite the fact that Cordell was well qualified and despite the fact that N956C was lightly loaded and operating perfectly, the airplane crashed well beyond the airport. The explosion could be seen for more than a mile. Cordell, alone in the airplane, died. As usual, the wreckage revealed only that Cordell had become spatially disoriented. There was no other explanation.

On December 1, 1964, Robert Anderson, a 36-year-old commercial pilot and one passenger, Miss Jean Tutor, 28, left Chicago Meigs Field for a business trip to Terre Haute, Ind. Anderson had more than 4000 hours' experience. He was operating Piper PA-30, N7057Y,[7] in accordance with Instrument Flight Rules. His clearance directed him to turn eastward after takeoff and climb to 3000 feet over Lake Michigan.

Two minutes after departure, N7057Y should have been nearing its assigned 3000-foot altitude. Anderson should have been talking to Chicago Departure Control on his radio. Instead, his radios were silent. He was cruising at high speed only ten feet above the water when he crashed, according to the last observer, the captain of the tug *Annie G.* Searchers went directly to the spot. No trace of N7057Y has ever been found.

Miss Tutor's body floated in three months later.

An important note concerning this accident is that Anderson had flown through a blinding blizzard in N7057Y to get to Meigs Field. The weather on his departure was comparatively good. If investigators had doubts about Anderson's ability that day they were dispelled by Anderson himself through his arrival in Chicago.

At 2:06 A.M., on December 30, 1964, a 48,000-pound airliner operated by Zantop Air Transport, Inc., arrived in the Detroit area with its crew and a load of auto parts. The weather was calm but dreary—a 200-foot ceiling and about one mile's visibility. But the Curtis Wright C-46A was a good airplane, and the crew was highly qualified. In fact, the pilot had more than 21,000 hours' experience, and the copilot had 2000 hours. The pilot was Capt. Alfred Oliver Fallon. His first officer was Hugo Lin Bair. Sitting directly behind them in jump seats was a relief crew, Capt. Dale R. Grisham and First Officer Ronald Reed.

The approach was not dangerous. It was nothing to be concerned about. They had made the same approach in worse weather many times before. It was 2:06 A.M. Detroit Approach Control, using radar, guided Zantop Flight 12/494[8] to the final approach course.

An Instrument Landing System is a very precise kind of radio navigation aid that can guide a pilot right down to within a few hundred feet of the centerline. It was an Instrument Landing System approach that Zantop 12/494 began at 2:06 A.M. Six minutes later the captain reported crossing the outer marker five miles from the end of the runway. He was descending northeast along the Instrument Landing System approach for a straight-in landing on the runway that points northeast. But according to the airport radar, Zantop 12/494 had gotten slightly to the left of the Instrument Landing System course. It was a normal error, but the controller called attention to it. Captain Fallon acknowledged.

Then something extraordinary happened.

The incredulous controller watched his radar display as Zantop 12/494 began a left turn of what was later calculated to be more than 60 degrees bank. That kind of bank is considered an aerobatic maneuver—not the sort of thing one does on an Instrument Landing System approach in actual instrument weather conditions with a 24-ton airplane.

The subsequent investigation of the crash was thorough. There was nothing wrong with the airplane before impact. There was nothing wrong with the Instrument Landing System on the ground. There were four pilots, any one of whom could have made the approach by himself.

The probable cause of the accident was "loss of control . . . for an undetermined reason."

The authorities had a more definite reason worked out early in the investigation. It didn't pan out, as they explained:

The abrupt, excessive, and abnormally steep turn, wholly inconsistent with a highly qualified instrument pilot making an ILS [Instrument Landing System] approach in instrument weather, suggests the possibility the captain, who was in the left seat, became suddenly incapacitated. The obvious partial recovery just before impact is *not* consistent with the possibility.

Aside from the problem noted therein, the medical authorities who specialize in accident investigation refused to go along. According to the doctors who examined the four bodies, Captain Fallon should have been perfectly able to perform his duties until impact. Even if that were not the case, there was still an experienced, instrument-qualified 30-year-old copilot already at the controls ready to take over, not to mention the extra crew sitting directly behind the two.

Meteorological factors were considered and dismissed.

Such cases clearly illustrate that *over the Great Lakes experienced pilots flying "on instruments" sometimes cannot control their airplanes.*

Chapter Eleven:

LOSS OF CONTROL ON VISUAL REFERENCE

Over the Great Lakes there have been hundreds of accidents in which qualified pilots at the controls of sound airplanes in calm air have lost control of their aircraft. Unlike previously discussed cases, these are not attributed to spatial disorientation, because they occurred in the clear, where, of course, spatial disorientation is not possible.

CF-FRC,[1] a Canadian-registered Cessna 310F, left Kenora in far-western Ontario at 7:15 P.M. for a trip across the length of Lake Superior to Sault Ste. Marie, Ont., on August 26, 1973. At the controls was an airline transport pilot with more than 13,000 hours' experience; more than 1500 of his hours were in Cessna 310s. The weather was beautiful throughout most of Canada, including CF-FRC's route that day, but the pilot filed an instrument flight plan. This would not normally be done in the United States, but it is a common safety practice in Canada.

CF-FRC was still 50 miles west of Sault Ste. Marie eastbound when Sault radar began painting its target. Shortly thereafter, the radar controller handed the aircraft to Kincheloe Air Force Base Approach Control. Kincheloe Approach, using radar, directed CF-FRC to a point on the Instrument Landing System course about five miles from the airport. From there the pilot could either follow his instruments right down the glide slope gently descending to the runway threshold, or he could make the approach visually, or he could do both. Making the approach visually was the most simple, since he could see the river banks on either side of him and the airport directly ahead. It was an easy approach.

But CF-FRC never made it to the airport. It descended, instead, slowly, with no sign of distress, into the river.

It was a gentle water landing for a landplane. As soon as it stopped moving all four occupants evacuated the airplane uninjured. This is known since all four crash victims were later found—drowned.

Descending into the river was a peculiar thing for CF-FRC to do. A Cessna 310 is not a cumbersome unresponsive airplane like the heavy jets that sometimes crash short of the threshold. Besides, CF-FRC touched down more than three miles from the airport at a point where it should have been 1000 feet above the water.

The thorough investigation that followed showed that all flight controls and engines on CF-FRC were working properly up until impact. All instruments and navigation radios in the airplane were functioning normally. The navigation aids on the ground were operating accurately. Nearby witnesses confirmed that the airport was clearly visible from the crash site at the time of the accident. The pilot was not incapacitated before impact—or even immediately after impact, for that matter. Everything aboard CF-FRC was as it should be.

Just as implausible were the events that overtook United Airlines Flight 389[2] somewhere over Lake Michigan on August 16, 1965.

This was a Boeing 727 operating on a regularly scheduled flight out of New York City's LaGuardia Airport. As usual there were three pilots in the cockpit that day. The captain was Melville W. Towle, 42, with more than 17,000 hours' experience. His copilot was Roger Marshall Whitezell, 34, with more than 8000 hours' experience. Their flight engineer, Maurice L. Femmer, 26, had 1000 hours' piloting experience. All three were fully rated commercial instrument pilots.

Towle, Whitezell, Femmer, three stewardesses and 24 passengers died that evening in what has become one of the strangest disasters in history.

The National Transportation Safety Board had dozens of accident investigators and scientists studying the sensational, widely publicized air disaster for two and a half years before the board, on January 10, 1968, quietly released its findings long after the public had forgotten the tragedy.

The board's announcement: There was no plausible way to explain what happened.

Briefly, here is what is recorded:

The flight was uneventful from New York City La-Guardia through Cleveland Center. At 9:02 P.M., on August 16, Cleveland Center handed off United 389 to Chicago Center. United 389 was proceeding smoothly westward at flight level 350 (this was 35,000 feet above sea level, since the barometric pressure was 29.92 inches). Chicago Center told Towle his plane was in radar contact and was cleared to the Pullman, Mich., radio fix, and from there to the Northbrook, Ill., radio fix, and from there to O'Hare International Airport.

United 389 acknowledged the clearance.

But between Pullman and Northbrook lies the width of Lake Michigan. That is only 13 minutes for a Boeing 727—even if the jet is slowing for entry into the Chicago Terminal Area as United 389 was.

United 389 left the eastern shore of Lake Michigan.

United 389 never made it to the western shore.

The weather was excellent. Towle, like the other two pilots, could see Chicago already.

It was just a few seconds past 9:20 P.M. that several witnesses saw the fireball on Lake Michigan. It seemed to leap upward from the gentle lake surface. Then it mushroomed out, lighting Chicago's clear eastern sky.

Several thousand pounds of floating material were recovered from the lake in the three days following the accident. It revealed little. Then 19 days after the crash, on September 2, the main wreckage was discovered. All the bodies and almost all the wreckage from the flight were recovered. Not recovered was the flight data recorder—that would have shown where the airplane was at every moment preceding the disaster.

However, the missing flight data recorder led authorities to what at the time seemed like a tremendous stroke of luck. The U.S. Air Force Air Defense Command (NORAD) maintains an extensive radar network along U.S. borders. The radar returns are fed into a highly sophisticated computer. The computer operates on an incredibly complex program called SAGE. The initials stand for "Semi-Automatic Ground Environment," although the acronym—an English word in itself—reflects more the program's intellectual capacity. What SAGE does is digest the radar returns and track any target that meets certain criteria of speed, altitude, position and heading. These "tracks" are recorded.

SAGE showed two tracks over that part of Lake Michigan at the time of the accident. One was track AO39. The other was track KO47. Since United 389 was the only aircraft over that part of the lake at that time, the two tracks both were presumed to be United 389. SAGE had recorded track AO39 until three minutes before the accident, when it dropped that track for some unknown reason. Then a minute later, two minutes before the crash, it started taping track KO47. There were some problems with correlating KO47 with United 389. The problems will be discussed later. But fortunately, all the SAGE data needed to trace United 389 was recorded on track AO39.

There were four important sources of information that made it possible for accident investigators to reconstruct exactly what led to the crash of United 389. First was the SAGE record of track AO39. Second was Chicago Center's taped record in Captain Towle's voice making United 389's position and altitude reports. This tape shows the exact time for each report. Third was the air traffic controllers' recollection of the radar track of United 389. And fourth was the precise weather information provided by the crew of a Boeing 707 which was flying approximately the same course five minutes behind United 389.

United 389, flying level at about 35,000 feet, was about eight minutes from Lake Michigan when Chicago Center cleared it down to flight level 230 (about 23,000 feet). United 389 was in the clear with the stars and moon above and a blanket of white below until five minutes east of Lake Michigan. There they penetrated the top of the cloud layer. That meant they were on instruments. They had not yet descended to Flight Level 230 when Chicago Center cleared them to continue descent past flight level 230 on down to 14,000 feet.

United 389 was at about 22,000 feet when it left the eastern shore of Lake Michigan westbound. That same minute, Chicago Center cleared United 389 all the way down to 6000 feet. Captain Towle acknowledged each one of the clearances, including the one instructing him to level off at 6000 feet. United 389 was under perfect control descending at about 2000 feet per minute. About three minutes before the accident, United 389 broke out of the clouds about 35 nautical (40 statute) miles from the Chicago shoreline. All three pilots could see the city lights and they could see the water clearly below. About two minutes before the crash, United 389 reached its assigned altitude. Until this point the course of events involving United 389 was perfectly normal. Then something unusual happened.

United 389 did not level off.

It continued descent. This is not a common mistake. It was a serious error that should have been noticed by all three pilots. It is not the sort of thing that ordinarily happens in an airplane cockpit. It is nevertheless possible though improbable that three pilots could overlook the situation for a few moments.

What happened three minutes later is far more improbable.

Only seconds away from death, with the lake surface rushing up toward him, his copilot flying the airplane, Captain Towle was engaged in a relaxed conversation with Chicago Approach Control about—of all things—his *altimeter setting*. Captain Towle was in the process of setting his altimeter, calmly speaking to Chicago Approach Control and staring straight at the warning hashmarks that told him he was about to die, and all while Lake Michigan closed in on his field of vision outside the cockpit.

While it is incredible that three pilots could overlook

both independent altimeter systems, it is even more implausible that they would fly a Boeing 727 and 30 souls to their death in Lake Michigan while all three could see their intended destination, the city of Chicago, 20 miles away.

These are the facts of the case. Given the information available, this was the way it *had* to have happened. Yet it is not possible.

As previously noted, the National Transportation Safety Board pondered the problem for two and a half years. Their final report sums up the dilemma:

> No reasonable explanation for their [the crew's] failure to level the aircraft at 6000 feet, their assigned altitude, can be offered. This is particularly true when one considers the fact that the last communication from the flight which ended at 2120:03 [three seconds past 9:20 P.M.] made reference to the altimeter setting.

Mentioned earlier was a problem associated with SAGE track KO47. The accident investigators had to conclude that track KO47 was the track of United 389 because there was no other air traffic in the area. Track KO47 began two minutes before the crash at a point just a few miles east of the crash site. The track moved westward along the same path at the same speed as United 389 right up to within 200 feet of where the wreckage was ultimately found.

The problem with correlating track KO47 with United 389 was quite serious, however. Track KO47 continued for two minutes after the crash of United 389 to a point 20 nautical (23 statute) miles due west of where the wreckage was later discovered. This would mean that the target on which track KO47 was reporting would have to have undergone a phenomenal acceleration. The target last reported by SAGE to be moving at 338 knots (390 miles per hour) would have to have accelerated to well above Mach 1, the speed of sound, in order to make good the position and time coordinates reported by SAGE.

In a report classified secret to this day, the Air Traffic Control group chairman explained that the information that the air defense radar fed into SAGE must have been erroneous. Track KO47 *had* to be United 389 because there just was absolutely no other air traffic in the area.

To suggest that track KO47 was anything besides United 389 would raise a serious question beyond the scope of the National Transportation Safety Board's investigation or responsibility. The question?

What was track KO47?

One of the most famous voyages in the history of the Great Lakes was the passage of the steamer *Alpena*[3] the night of October 15 and 16, 1880. She was last seen on course at about the same place United 389 passed through its assigned altitude, 6000 feet.

The *Alpena* was a posh freight and passenger ship of the Goodrich line. Normally the steamer would load freight at Muskegon, Mich., in the late afternoon and early evening. Then it would steam 12 miles south to Grand Haven, Mich., where it would take on the rest of its cargo and passengers for its nightly trip southwest across Lake Michigan to Chicago. En route it would pass the *Muskegon*, another Goodrich ship that made the same route on alternate nights. The *Alpena* would arrive Chicago early in the morning, begin unloading and loading, and head back to Muskegon the following night.

The *Alpena* departed Grand Haven at 10:00 P.M. promptly as scheduled for her trip to Chicago on October 15. Reports vary, but there were somewhere between 60 and 101 people aboard. Several ships subsequently noted the *Alpena's* passage.

These reports are extremely difficult to reconcile.

First, her sister ship the *Muskegon* passed her in mid-lake halfway to Chicago at 1:00 A.M. on October 16. The *Alpena* was pushing along at full steam toward Chicago. The ships sounded their company salute as they passed in opposite directions. This was normal. Nothing was amiss.

But then, at 3:00 A.M., the schooner *Challenger* saw the *Alpena*. The *Alpena* was only about 35 miles from Chicago, headed on course. The ship was all right, except for one thing. By 3:00 A.M. she should already have docked in Chicago.

The next sighting, for which no explanation has ever been offered, was by the *S. A. Irish*, a barge that was being towed to Milwaukee. The *Alpena* followed the barge for three hours early the morning of October 16. This was far north of the *Alpena's* intended course, and the *Alpena* was traveling away from her intended destination.

At noon, on October 16, the *Alpena* was traveling in company with the schooner *Grand Haven*. When they parted, they were only five miles from Racine, Wisc., far north of the *Alpena's* destination. The *Alpena* could have safely turned into Racine had there been a problem, but when the *Grand Haven* last saw her she was headed out toward midlake.

That afternoon, the schooner *Levi Grant* passed within one and a half miles of the *Alpena* somewhere northeast of Racine. Aside from this inexplicable location, the report contained another strange element. The *Alpena's* wheels were turning, and her steam whistle was sounding. Steam was coming from her engines. That was as it should be.

But there was no smoke from her stacks.

There was no fire under her boiler.

The *Alpena* was not indicating any distress.

"Vanished" is the word used to describe what the *Alpena* did next. It is used by every historian who has studied the case.

Presumably all those aboard died.

No survivors and no wreck have ever been found.

In 1964 the Holland, Mich., airport, on the east shore of Lake Michigan, had no precision approaches. James Taylor and Andre Docos, both experienced pilots, wanted to practice making Instrument Landing System approaches, so, on April 29, 1964, they flew 30 miles north along the shoreline to Muskegon, Mich., where Muskegon County Airport has an Instrument Landing System. The weather was good. The ceiling was 8000 feet, visibility was five miles and wind was steady out of the south at 12 knots (14 miles per hour).

To practice instrument approaches in good weather,

two pilots are required. One pilot wears a view-limiting device that works like a pair of blinders. The device prevents him from seeing anything outside the cockpit. This simulates instrument conditions in the clouds where the pilot has no visual reference outside the cockpit. The second pilot, the safety pilot, must watch for other air traffic to make sure the practice flight does not interfere with visual flights which are free to operate without clearances from Air Traffic Control.

It was 7:30 P.M. when Taylor and Docos left Holland in N7989X,[4] a well equipped Cessna 172. They arrived at Muskegon 15 minutes later and spent the next hour practicing Instrument Landing System approaches and holding patterns. Then they landed and ate dinner at the Muskegon County Airport restaurant. After dinner, at 9:30 P.M., they were cleared once again to fly five miles east of the airport, turn around, and fly the Instrument Landing System approach.

Shortly after takeoff the air traffic control tower operator watched N7989X disappear.

The weather was deteriorating, so the tower controller asked N7989X if it had flown into the clouds or if its navigation lights had been turned off. N7989X answered negative on both counts. As far as Taylor and Docos were concerned they still should be clearly visible to the tower. But they were not. The tower asked for their altitude. They said 1100 feet and added that they were descending and that *they could see clearly everything beneath them*. They were still 500 feet above the water. They knew this. One pilot was watching outside the cockpit. The other was watching the instruments.

David B. Wilson, a 47-year-old inspection foreman, was fishing that night—dipping for smelt to be precise—when he saw an airplane descending "lower and lower," as he put it. The airplane descended into Lake Michigan. "The visibility was good at this time," Wilson said.

N7989X never indicated there was a problem. The only thing the tower controller knew was that he could not get a response when he tried to contact the airplane.

On May 10, most of the wreckage was brought up in a large fishnet. It was 1300 feet from shore. On May 12,

Taylor's body was found. An autopsy showed no incapacitating condition. On June 6, a diver found the aircraft engine and propeller. Everything was examined closely. There was fuel in the tanks. The engine had suffered no pre-impact damage. Neither had the airframe or flight controls.

Unlike most of the others, this accident was not recorded "probable cause undetermined." The official cause of this accident was a masterful understatement. "The pilot misjudged his altitude resulting in descent into the lake," said the accident brief. There is little question this is true. However, it does not go far toward an understanding of the cause of the tragedy. Why did two experienced pilots flying in the clear in a perfectly functioning airplane descend to their deaths in Lake Michigan? No answer to this question has been proposed.

Two experienced commercial pilots were at the controls of DeHavilland DHC1B2, registration number CF-CXT,[5] on July 29, 1956, in the middle of the afternoon when witnesses watched it flying over Kister Board, Niagara Falls. The two were engaged in mutual instructor training. Weather was good.

Witnesses later reported that "the aircraft dived at a steep angle and one [witness] stated that he saw the aircraft make a steep bank to the left and strike the ground."

Examination of the wreckage revealed that the flight controls were working properly on impact. The engines were developing substantial power when they made ground contact.

One of the two pilots survived. He could not remember the flight.

The Canadian authorities who investigated the crash labeled its cause "undetermined."

R. Wilson was an experienced pilot with some 1000 hours at the controls July 17, 1960, he was flying sky-divers in CF-HHD.[6] He had taken F. Martineau and J. McCutcheon up for a jump and was returning to Welland Airport between Lake Erie and Lake Ontario when the following occurred:

The aircraft went into a steep dive and struck the ground short of the runway. The pilot was killed and the aircraft was destroyed.

It was established that the aircraft struck the ground in an attitude past the vertical. A thorough inspection of the flight controls was carried out and they were found to be functioning normally. . . .

For an undetermined reason the aircraft dived into the ground during the approach for landing.

The twin-engine Aerostar 601 is known for its aerodynamic efficiency and responsive controls. John J. Fair, a 38-year-old professional pilot with more than 6000 hours' experience, was at the controls of just such an airplane, N8MW,[7] about sunup on October 3, 1973. He was carrying 29,000 canceled checks from Cleveland to Chicago banks. The flight was on an instrument flight plan until Fair saw his destination airport, Meigs Field. With the airport clearly in sight, he canceled the instrument flight plan and said he would continue visually. Still almost a minute from the airport, Fair flew the Aerostar 601 into Lake Michigan two miles from the runway with such speed that the gasoline in the wingtanks exploded, sending flames 40 feet high. Subsequent investigation showed that Fair was not incapacitated and that N8MW was functioning properly prior to impact. Aerodynamically at least, N8MW was in fully controlled flight when it descended into Lake Michigan.

Delton Pangle was in a car northeast of Three Rivers, Mich., about 40 miles east of southern Lake Michigan, on July 16, 1968. Mrs. Tempie Delmore was fishing in a river not far away. Both witnessed the last minutes in the life of pilot Charles N. Neblock, 52, of Vicksberg, Mich.

It had been a beautifully clear afternoon when Neblock took off in the Cessna 150, registration N2969S.[8] The plane was in normal level flight when it pitched downward 90 degrees and descended vertically into the wooded area. Subsequent examination of the wreckage by the experts showed no mechanical failure prior to impact. Neblock's autopsy disclosed no factors significant to the cause of the accident. Once again, the airplane was aerodynamically under control when it dove to the surface.

This has happened hundreds of times over and around the Great Lakes.

Roy Dychakowsky took off from Parry Sound, Ont., at 4:45 P.M., September 30, 1960. Parry Sound is on the eastern shore of Georgian Bay of Lake Huron. The next day, the aircraft, a Republic RC3, registration CF-DKF,[9] was found where it had hit the ground in a near-vertical attitude. Dychakowsky was dead. The Republic RC3 was destroyed. A thorough investigation followed.

The results showed that the weather was excellent. The pilot suffered no pre-impact physical incapacity. There was no pre-impact problem with the engine, airframe or controls. As usual a fully functioning airplane with a qualified pilot at the controls simply dove to its total destruction. The Canada Department of Transport summed up the investigation nicely: "The aircraft struck the ground in a nearly vertical attitude for reasons which could not be determined."

N11Q,[10] a Wittman Tailwind, took off from Waunakee, Wisc., west of Lake Michigan, at 5:00 P.M. on March 26, 1961. About 15 minutes later it crashed, killing the pilot and his only passenger. The government investigators were able to assign a cause to the accident. It was "inflight structural failure caused by a high speed maneuver during which forces exceeded the structural ultimate load factor."

However, this probable cause raised more questions than it answered. The commercial pilot flying N11Q had put the aircraft into an incredibly high-power, high-speed dive, so drastic that it overstressed the airframe and caused the airplane to disintegrate before it ever got to the ground. No suggestion is made in the accident report on why a 27-year-old experienced pilot with more than 1500 hours at the controls would intentionally do this.

A similarly odd explanation was assigned to the crash of N6298X,[11] a large Aero Commander 500B. The lightly loaded airplane took off from Rochester, N.Y., just south of Lake Ontario, early on the morning of March 3, 1972, and crashed shortly thereafter. The National Transportation Safety Board called it a stall that resulted from the pilot's failure to maintain flying speed. But the pilot was an airline-transport-rated professional with more than 3000 hours' experience, including more than 500 hours in airplanes like the one that killed him. Such a mistake is far too elementary to routinely assign to a pilot with that experience.

Similarly, the National Transportation Safety Board said that the probable cause of the May 19, 1969, crash of a Piper PA-20, registration N7604K,[12] was Donald E. DeMott's failure to maintain flying speed. The board did not suggest a reason why DeMott, an airline-transport-rated pilot with more than 7000 hours, including 125 hours in PA-20s, would inadvertently stall one while on final approach to a major airport like Timmerman at Milwaukee, Wisc., on the western shore of Lake Michigan. This is an exceedingly strange way for an experienced professional pilot to end his life in an airplane as gentle as the PA-20.

Another question that the official explanation failed to answer deals with the airplane's altitude at the beginning of the stall. Several witnesses reported it variously from 700 to 1000 feet above the ground. This would have been adequate altitude to recover from even the most drastic stall. Making the stall theory even more peculiar was the presence of another pilot in the copilot's seat. That was Carl E. Hill, who was a certified flight instructor himself, although he had somewhat less experience than DeMott.

Hill survived the accident but could remember nothing of the flight—nothing except for one very curious thing: He thought the flight controls were somehow frozen or unmovable before the crash.

Subsequent and thorough examination of the wreckage,

however, showed that the controls were working, and no evidence could be found of anything that might possibly have interfered with them before impact. Hill's recollection was discounted.

Authorities similarly admitted there was no explanation for the crash of N2657G,[13] a Cessna 182, on August 15, 1969, at Bay City, Mich., next to Lake Huron. N2657G made a fully controlled descent into a swamp, killing all aboard.

The same thing happened again two months later on October 26, 1969, at Middleport, N.Y., on the south shore of Lake Ontario. It happened to N2389V,[14] a Cessna 140. The National Transportation Safety Board admitted the fatal crash was unexplainable.

It was almost the same at Lawton, Mich., just west of Lake Michigan, on September 2, 1970. At 5:00 P.M. a pilot with more than 2500 hours suddenly and for no apparent reason lost control of his Waco ZGC-7, registration N2270,[15] and plummeted to earth. Probable cause remains "undetermined."

That was similar to what happened to the woman who took off from Port Perry, Ont., ten miles north of Lake Ontario, at 2:00 P.M., on May 23, 1971. It was a local flight and 45 minutes later witnesses on the ground saw the DeHavilland DHC1B2, registration CF-CYU,[16] making a slow but erratic uncontrolled descent. They watched it fly wide circles right up until the ground interrupted its descent. Official cause remains "undetermined."

The National Transportation Safety Board was likewise unable to determine why an airline transport flight instructor, his student and their Cessna 150, registration N4033J,[17] came tumbling out of the air on January 14, 1973. The pilot in command had over 1500 hours in Cessna 150s. Weather was good. There was no pre-impact failure of the aircraft.

How can so many of these strange tragedies happen in such proximity to the Great Lakes? Statistically, it is worth noting that the busy northeastern air corridors between Boston and Washington *do not even come close* in the number of such unexplained disasters.

Robert Ryan Ferris, a 45-year-old Chicago waiter, was a reasonably experienced private pilot. He left home on Valentine's Day, 1964, to do some shopping and get some kind of "city license." But the lines were so long that Ferris decided to go flying instead. He called his wife from Sky Harbor Airport about 4:00 P.M. and told her to have the children in the backyard around 4:30 P.M. when he planned to make a low pass over the house.

It is known that Ferris took off in a Cessna 150, registration N2030Z,[18] shortly after the conversation with his wife. It is also known that an airplane matching the description of N2030Z made a low pass over the Ferris home about 4:30 P.M. Such maneuvers frequently result in accidents by inexperienced pilots. But this airplane did not have an accident—at least not at 4:30 P.M.

Later other witnesses saw an airplane, also matching the description of N2030Z. It was over Lake Michigan not far from the Illinois shore. It was at a safe altitude.

Mats Johnson described subsequently what he saw next: "As it proceeded out over the lake it took a steep right turn to the south and entered a dive simultaneously." Lois C. Jorndt and Mrs. Ethel Johnson (no relation to Mats Johnson) reported seeing just about the same thing.

Ferris' body floated in to shore about two and a half months later.

No explanation has yet been proposed for the curious behavior of Ferris and N2030Z.

The list of examples could continue forever. It may do just that.

Chapter Twelve:

CREW INSANITY

Many of the unexplainable Great Lakes disasters have produced clear evidence of grossly irrational behavior by the affected crew.

One of the best-known examples is the loss of the schooner *George F. Whitney*.[1] It was recorded as follows by J. B. Mansfield in his description of the events of 1872:

Foundered in Mid-Lake.—The loss of the schooner *George F. Whitney*, in September, was a peculiar one. She must have foundered in mid-lake, as not one of the crew of eight men were ever heard of nor has the manner of her loss ever been known. Captain Carpenter was in command. A strange fatality seems to have hung over the *Whitney* for more than a year. She had been wrecked on Sugar Island on a trip from Buffalo to Chicago in 1871: was released in the spring of 1872, and reconstructed, and on her first trip she was wrecked again at Vermilion. During the next voyage she was lost with all on board. It was said that while lying at dock at Chicago, Captain Carpenter displayed all his flags at halfmast, the American ensign with union down. Upon inquiry why he did this the captain explained that it was merely an invitation for the tugs to transfer him up the river.

Almost 100 years later on October 16, 1963, about 8:30 A.M., a Piper PA-24, registration N7544P,[2] was flying south of Toledo near the western end of Lake Erie. Weather was good. The pilot was a professional, highly experienced in the PA-24.

The Piper PA-24 has four fuel tanks. There is a main

and auxiliary tank in each wing. The pilot draws on the fuel tank of his choice by moving the fuel selector to the appropriate position. On this particular morning over northwestern Ohio, N7544P's engine was drawing fuel from the right auxiliary wing tank. When that tank burned dry, the engine stopped running. This was no problem for an experienced professional pilot. The airplane continued gliding forward with the propeller windmilling. All that needed to be done was to move the fuel selector to another tank. In this case, any tank would do.

But the pilot of N7544P did a most peculiar thing. He began gliding down toward an open field as though his only alternative were a forced landing. At the last minute he saw some high-tension wires and in trying to avoid them, he stalled N7544P, destroying it and killing himself. Investigation of the wreckage baffled the experts. The fuel selector switch was still on the right auxiliary tank. That a professional pilot could watch his engine stop from fuel exhaustion and fail to switch tanks is absolutely inconceivable. As in all such cases, the possibility of pre-impact incapacitation of the pilot is raised. But the investigation produced no such evidence. There is little to be said of such accidents. There is some reason —there has to be some reason—why the pilot of N7544P failed to switch fuel tanks. No one knows what it could be.

I have made only a few parachute jumps in my life, but I know the wonderful feeling of security that comes just after an opening shock when the parachutist looks up to see a perfectly round canopy supporting him. It is the kind of security to which one clings.

Shelly Francis O'Neil was sport-parachuting near Damascus, Ont., on September 8, 1974, near the eastern shore of Lake Huron. She got a good opening shock and a good canopy at about 2000 feet above the ground. Then she did something very odd.

She released the canopy.

As she plummeted downward she could have deployed her reserve parachute. She had more than ten seconds to do it. She didn't.

The immediate cause of death was evident. No one

has been able to explain why she released the good canopy, and failed to deploy her reserve.

The crash of N1252P on September 6, 1964, has already been discussed (see Chapter Six). It was the twin-engine Piper that for no apparent reason lost an engine and crashed within sight of Howell Airport just south of Chicago on the western shore of Lake Michigan. Laboratory analysis of the combustion-chamber deposits showed that both engines were capable of producing normal power prior to impact. Even though the three pilots were behaving as though they had an engine failure, there was no evidence to indicate that such a situation existed. But there are some other things that made the crash of N1252P extraordinary.

First, a single engine failure on that airplane, loaded the way it was, should not have caused a forced landing. The airplane was perfectly capable of maintaining or increasing its altitude with the remaining engine. Even if N1252P had lost an engine, returning to Howell on the remaining engine was a simple matter. But N1252P did a number of crazy things, unexplained to this day.

For one, the pilot lowered the landing gear. This greatly increased the drag on the airplane and greatly reduced its single-engine performance. Next he began a descent as though he were preparing to land immediately. The airport was only a few miles away. Then, with two other pilots in the airplane, he slowed the craft until he could no longer maintain control. The result was total destruction of the airplane and death to all aboard.

In stark implausibility, the actions of the crew aboard the *Marquette & Bessemer No. 2*[3] on her last voyage are without equal. The *No. 2* was a car ferry, a ship built to carry railroad cars from one railhead to another. Specifically, the *No. 2* made a daily shuttle between Port Stanley, Ont., on the north shore of Lake Erie and Conneaut, Ohio, on the south shore. Since the car ferries tried to maintain regular schedules, they were unusually sturdy ships built for all kinds of weather. The *No. 2* was 350 feet long. She could carry 30 railroad cars, each weighing 30 tons. Capt. Robert McLeod was the master—a man of unquestioned ability. McLeod's older brother, John, had been offered his own command but chose instead to serve as younger brother Robert's first mate. The second mate of the *No. 2* was Frank Stone, who at 25 was the youngest man on the lakes holding a full commission as a ship's pilot. He had won the commission with an unusually high grade on the examination.

Some unusual things involving the crew of the *No. 2* happened for several days preceding the December 7, 1909, run from Conneaut to Port Stanley.

John Clancy was the *No. 2's* wheelsman. His family lived in Erie, Pa. On December 4, 1909, his sister, Sarah Clancy, became hysterical. She was the victim of a vivid and terrible nightmare. In that terrifying dream, she saw a ship sinking in a storm, and throughout the vision, she could hear her brother John's voice. It was, in fact, those dreadful cries for help that panicked her.

On December 7, 1909, deckhand John Wirtz wrote a curious letter to his family in Saginaw, Mich. It may seem less curious to those who have never sailed, but professional seamen who live and work on their shipboard homes are normally quite comfortable at sea. The *No. 2* in fact was just a ferry making a daily run across the lake. Wirtz had written that he was in constant fear for his life. "The next trip will be my last," the letter said.

Fireman Tom Steele had made plans for the December 7 trip to be his last. He had found a shore job and was scheduled to begin work right away.

When several other hands left the ship, crew shortages prompted chief engineer Eugene Wood to send porter George L. Lawrence on December 7 to search for men to add to the black gang. Lawrence by coincidence met his girlfriend on the street, and she induced him to miss the trip. (Incidentally, Engineer Wood was the brother of George Wood, who had been master of the steamer *Bannockburn* when it vanished on Lake Superior in 1902. See Chapter Two).

When circumstances removed two more from the regu-

138

lar crew, it seemed as if some strange force was selectively thinning the crew of the *No. 2*.

There was another curious event that preceded the scheduled sailing on December 7. Captain McLeod received instructions from his company that the car ferry, which normally did not carry passengers, was to transport a rather mysterious man from Erie, Pa., across the lake. McLeod actually had to bring the ship back to the dock to pick the man up when he arrived a few minutes late. The passenger was Albert J. Weiss, and although no one knew it at the time, the nattily dressed man had in his brown briefcase $50,000 in cash for a strange business transaction that was to take place in Canada.

At 10:43 P.M. on December 7, the *No. 2* headed from the river channel into Lake Erie with 26 cars of coal, three cars of structural steel and one car of iron castings.

A few miles out, the *No. 2* passed the tug *Albert T*. The tug captain, Frank Snyder, said that as he passed the *No. 2*, Captain McLeod for no apparent reason came out of the pilot house and began speaking to the *Albert T*. through a megaphone. But Snyder and his crew could hear nothing as McLeod spoke.

On the afternoon of December 7, a Canadian customs officer named Wheeler said he saw the *No. 2* a few miles from her destination, Port Stanley. But he said she turned back into the lake.

That night of December 7, a woman heard a whistle that she recognized as the *No. 2*. As she later reported, she saw the ship's light heading directly for shore. She averted this catastrophe by showing a light herself. The *No. 2* made a left turn safely back toward the lake, she said.

Another woman, Mrs. James Holland, and her son, who lived near Fairview, west of Erie, Pa., heard distress signals that night. That was at 7:00 P.M. and again at midnight.

At 1:30 A.M., December 8, at Conneaut Harbor, William Rice was standing outside the cab of the huge ore unloader that he operated. He heard what he recognized to be the *No. 2's* whistle. He paid particular attention to it because she was blowing distress signals—four short blasts each. After five consecutive distress calls, she signaled that she was dropping anchor. Then she began the distress calls. They lasted 15 minutes, then stopped. The details of this report were confirmed by a fellow worker and a local man, A. G. Brebner, who also knew the *No. 2's* whistle. Try as they did, they could not see the *No. 2* or her lights.

Both the master and the chief engineer of the steamer *Black*, however, reported seeing the *No. 2* near Conneaut Harbor that night.

The reports that she was on the south side of Lake Erie contradicted Canadian customs officer Wheeler's report that she was on the north side. It most certainly contradicted Wheeler's report that he heard the *No. 2's* whistle off the Port Stanley harbor entrance at 3:00 A.M. on December 8. Nevertheless, another Canadian living at Bruce, Ont., just seven miles east of Port Stanley confirmed what Wheeler said. He claimed to have heard the whistle so close to shore that he thought she had gone aground. He jumped out of bed, lighted a lantern, and went to investigate. He said he could hear the ship "as plain as day," but he was unable to see her.

Exactly where the *No. 2* was that night, or, for that matter, where she is today, has never been established, despite considerable study. The search continues because of the $50,000 that now belongs to the first person who can solve this everlasting mystery.

But what happened to the souls aboard the *No. 2* is an even more frightening story. On December 12, 1909, nine were found adrift in a lifeboat 15 miles off Erie, Pa. The Pennsylvania State Fish Commissioner's tug, *Commodore Perry*, spotted the men on the horizon. One lay on the bottom of the boat but the others were still upright at the oars. To this day no one knows how long they had been adrift, or exactly when their ship disappeared. The men themselves were little help solving the mystery, for as the *Commodore Perry* neared it became horribly apparent that they were frozen, all of them, dead in their seats.

Stranger still were the clothes of a tenth man. *The Cleveland Plain Dealer* reported as follows:

In the bow end of the boat was found complete clothing for one man, and it is the belief that the yawl originally contained ten men and that one, becoming crazed, had discarded his clothing and jumped into the icy waters of Lake Erie.

Equally puzzling was that the ship's cook, frozen in the lifeboat with the others, was carrying two long galley knives and a meat cleaver—useless tools in a lifeboat on Lake Erie. The boat didn't even have enough oars. All the men were lightly clad. There was no food. But the cook had brought two long knives and a meat cleaver.

One theory—although it is as insane as no theory at all—on the knives arose the next fall on October 6, 1910, when Captain McLeod's body was discovered. It bore two severe slash wounds.

The most plausible explanations of what happened on Lake Erie the night of December 7 and 8, 1909, involve some kind of mass insanity. But even those do not explain how or why the ship was at the northern and southern shores simultaneously. And it seems that no possible theory could ever explain the curious events that preceded the tragic voyage.

Chapter Thirteen:

MEMORY LOSS

There exists a large group of Great Lakes disasters involving inexplicable events that are survived by individuals who remember nothing of those events.

Richard G. deMontfort, 36, of Hamilton, Ont., left home on August 4, 1965, headed for Rockford, Ill., in his Mong Sport, registration CF-PNG,[1] a snappy light airplane that cruised at 110 miles per hour on about 25 miles per gallon. DeMontfort spent the night in Romeo, Mich., and began his second leg on August 5. DeMontfort planned to stop for fuel at Three Rivers, Mich., before heading around the tip of Lake Michigan to Rockford, Ill. He almost made it.

Just east of his destination, witness Wilbur Davis reported seeing the Mong Sport flying west at about 300 feet above the ground. That is unusually low, especially for the excellent weather that prevailed that day. Then Davis saw something even more peculiar. DeMontfort circled Davis' house at about 100 feet above the ground. This time the aircraft engine was sputtering. DeMontfort flew a short distance northwest and suddenly the engine quit and the plane plunged to the ground. The engine failure was not caused by running out of gas. There was still plenty of fuel in the tanks.

DeMontfort was not killed. The wreckage showed no pre-impact damage to the airframe, controls or engine. There was no apparent cause for the crash. Authorities sought from deMontfort the explanations that eluded them.

DeMontfort's survival did not aid the investigation. It only raised more questions. DeMontfort could remember nothing of the crash. He could remember nothing of the aimless circling. In fact, deMontfort could remember nothing after passing Detroit, Mich., more than 100 miles to the east between Lake Huron and Lake Erie. DeMontfort's mind had gone completely blank as he passed the Pontiac, Mich., radio navigation station.

Why did CF-PNG crash? DeMontfort knows only what the rest of us know. Nothing.

Braniff Airlines Flight 560[2] used to leave Dallas, Tex., in the middle of the night. It would stop in Oklahoma City, Wichita and Kansas City before arriving in Chicago about dawn. In July 1955, the flight was a Convair 340. And on July 17 the captain was Allen R. Tobin. The first officer was Orbin W. Hanks. The weather was beautiful except that there was some light fog at Chicago's Midway Airport, Braniff's 560's destination.

At 5:47 A.M., Chicago Center cleared Braniff 560 as follows:

ATC [Air Traffic Control] clears Braniff 560 to the Naperville Omni [a radio navigation fix] via Peoria, Victor 116 [an airway] over Joliet, maintain at least 1000 [feet] on top [of clouds]. Tops reported 2000 [feet above] msl [mean sea level]. Contact Chicago Center on 118.9 passing Peoria.

Braniff 560 acknowledged and reported crossing Peoria as instructed. At 6:18 A.M. Chicago Center handed off Braniff 560 to Chicago Midway Approach Control. And Chicago Approach gave Braniff 560 radar vectors (directions) to the Instrument Landing System course. Braniff 560 began what was later described as a very good approach by the air traffic controllers watching its progress on radar.

At 6:24 A.M. the sun was shining over Lake Michigan and Braniff 560 was demolished, killing Captain Tobin, stewardess Mary E. Teel and 40 passengers.

It was a curious accident, especially under the circumstances. According to the special weather observation at the time of the crash, Braniff 560's crew should have been able to see the runway and control the airplane even without the instruments. There was no indication that the Convair 340 was making its approach dangerously low and slow as is so often the case when airliners crash just short of the runway threshold. The Civil Aeronautics Board sought answers from the copilot, who survived the accident.

He could remember nothing of the accident.

In fact, he could remember nothing of the flight.

Several months after the accident, those few hours of his life were still a blank.

The Civil Aeronautics Board admitted that no positive determination was possible under the circumstances. They theorized, nevertheless, that after the crew had established visual contact with the runway, they unexpectedly encountered an area of fog that forced them to switch back to flying by instruments and they lost control in the time it took them to make the transition.

But the explanation is not satisfactory. While it does take more than a half-second to make the transition described by the board, it is not likely that the crew could "inadvertently" have entered the fog. This *can* happen at night, but Braniff 560 crashed well after sunrise. Captain Tobin should have been able to see anything he was flying into, anticipating any transition that was necessary.

Why did Braniff 560 crash? The answer is locked in the grave of Captain Tobin and the lost memory of First Officer Hanks. All available evidence indicates that the engines, controls, instruments and radios were working properly, as were the ground stations and approach lights to the runway.

Another even more implausible memory loss is the now famous story of Barney and Betty Hill.[3] The night of September 19, 1961, they were several miles east of Lake Ontario, returning from a vacation in Canada in their car through this lonely mountainous region, when they noticed a bright light in the sky. It skimmed along just above the ridgeline, staying even with their car for about 30 miles. Then it descended in front of them. Barney, a postal worker, eager to learn more about the curious light, grabbed his binoculars and headed for the craft. Mr. Hill's curiosity, however, lasted only until he saw strange humanoid characters staring down upon him from the windows of this odd vehicle. Seeing the crew of this mysterious vessel disturbed Hill enough that he commenced screaming that he was about to be captured, ran at full speed back to his car, jumped in and "we roared down the highway," explained his wife.

"Almost immediately we heard a strange series of beeping sounds and the car seemed to vibrate. We felt a heavy drowsiness come over us and Barney turned the car down a side road that turned out to be a dead end."

Two hours later the Hills found themselves 35 miles down the road, unable to remember what had happened or explain several things such as the stopping of their watches and strange scuffs on the car. Both Mr. and Mrs. Hill felt enough anxiety that by 1964 they sought help from Boston amnesia expert Dr. Benjamin Simon.

Simon hypnotized them separately and repeatedly. Under his trance, both vividly recalled that they had been taken aboard the vessel, whereupon the humanoids conducted thorough physical examinations. The leader even pointed out his homebase to Betty on a star chart.

No one knows, for various reasons, how many such encounters with UFOs have taken place in the Great Lakes region and how many tragedies have resulted.

UFOs notwithstanding, the Canada Department of Transport reports that on August 18, 1968, at 4:30 P.M., near Huddersfield Township, Ont., north of Lake Ontario and east of Lake Huron, aircraft CF-SCF,[4] a Bell 47G4 helicopter doing geological survey work, crashed. Killed in the accident was the pilot, an experienced commercial pilot with 730 hours in helicopters just like CF-SCF, including 186 hours in the previous 90 days.

Oddly enough, the passenger escaped the disaster with nothing more than minor injuries. After he was rescued in this desolate wilderness near the lakes, he told the authorities about how the helicopter seemed to be flying normally and then for no apparent reason began slowly descending until it struck the trees, rolled to the right and crashed.

This passenger found himself two hours later, alive and well.

He remembers nothing of what happened during those two hours.

Canadian scientists made a thorough examination of the wreckage, the pilot's body, the weather and the strange report from the surviving passenger.

There was no reason for the crash.

Their conclusion as to probable cause was one word: "undetermined."

N3570R,[5] a Beechcraft 23 on the Canadian side of Sioux Narrows between Lake Huron and Lake Superior, started the same kind of unusual landing not too long after takeoff at 11:40 A.M., August 28, 1966. Fortunately there were no trees in this case. The aircraft was not destroyed and no one was killed. Nevertheless, the Canadian authorities launched the same kind of thorough examination of the case.

The pilot was of little help. He could remember nothing.

Neither were the witnesses on the ground who watched the strange event. Nor was the damaged aircraft itself at all revealing. Again, there was no reason for the accident. Probable cause was simply "undetermined."

Similarly, the lone man who survived Otis Redding's fatal crash (see Chapter Six) could remember nothing of it, even though he was not seriously injured.

Near Grand Bend, Ont., on the southeast shore of Lake Huron, CF-PEF,[6] a Piper PA-18, came gliding across an open field, its engine idling as though it were being forced to make an emergency landing. That was on July 5, 1963, at 7:22 P.M. CF-PEF crashed into the trees at the edge of the field. Neither the pilot, J. F. Grieve, of Wyoming, Ont., an experienced private pilot, nor his only passenger, E. South of Watford, Ont., were killed.

In this case investigators didn't have to break down the engine to find that nothing was wrong. It still ran perfectly after the crash. There were no other problems— no structural failure, no pilot incapacitation, no bad weather.

As for the two survivors, they remembered nothing of the accident. Not only that, they remembered nothing of the flight—neither of them. Grieve and South know less about their own journey than the witnesses who watched its dramatic and unexpected end.

The evidence left the Canada Department of Transport with little choice. The probable cause of the accident was recorded as follows: "For reasons that could not be determined, the aircraft struck trees during flight at low altitude."

Chapter Fourteen:

FORESEEN EVENTS

There exists a list of tragedies—not long but exceedingly difficult to comprehend—in which principals, for no apparent reason, foresaw catastrophic events on the Great Lakes.

The *Waubuno's*[1] November 22, 1879, journey from Collingwood, Ont., in Georgian Bay is one of the most often told stories of the Great Lakes. Virtually all latter-day historians of the region have studied and written about this event, which, though it contains an element of fantasy, is nevertheless quite true.

The *Waubuno* was a relatively new steamer. She had been built in 1865. Despite the thorough research, no one seems to know why she got the name *Waubuno*. It was a peculiar name for a ship. It was an Algonquin (Indian) name for those who practice the blackest of arts. To the Algonquins there were only a few Waubunos but they were men to be feared. They could cast horrible spells on their enemies—and from these spells there was said to be no escape whatsoever. In retrospect, the name *Waubuno* has become even more unsettling.

Mrs. W. D. Doupe was in her cabin aboard the *Waubuno* in Collingwood harbor on November 20, 1879, when she had a most disturbing vision. What she saw was the *Waubuno* wrecked, with her husband, herself and fellow passengers drowning in the icy waters of Lake Huron. That vision was sufficiently realistic that Mrs. Doupe, who claimed no psychic powers, became hysterical and refused to sail on the ship. Presumably this caused her husband great consternation. He was a doctor who had just completed his medical training. The newlywed couple was headed north to the remote McKeller Village, Ont. Dr. Doupe's calmer head prevailed, and his wife was sent to her cabin to get some sleep. Before she retired, however, Mrs. Doupe caused great anxiety among the other passengers, to each of whom she gave an unsettling description of his own upcoming death.

Though Mrs. Doupe was intent on postponing her destiny, the *Waubuno's* captain, George Burkett, seemed anxious to get to his. At that moment his destination was Parry Sound, Ont. On November 21, he told the passengers that the *Waubuno* planned to sail the following day. Consequently, many of the would-be passengers went ashore to stay with friends or in the hotel at Collingwood. However, at 3:30 A.M., on November 22, Captain Burkett sent ship's purser John Rowland into town to rouse the passengers who could be located. Some made it. Some narrowly missed the boat. There were ten passengers and 14 crew members warmly tucked away in the *Waubuno* when she pulled away somewhat unexpectedly at 4:00 A.M., thereby missing a small contingent of angry citizens left shouting on the dock as they watched their ship sail away.

People along Georgian Bay found the thousands and thousands of apples the *Waubuno* carried. They found a lifeboat. And despite enormous improbability, they found every single lifejacket that had been carried aboard the ship. Ultimately they even found the *Waubuno's* hull, badly battered by some tremendous force—just as Mrs. Doupe had foreseen. It was barely afloat, still in Georgian Bay.

But they never found Mrs. Doupe's body.

They never found that of her husband, Dr. Doupe.

In fact, not a soul aboard the *Waubuno*—not a single body—has ever been seen since.

Consequently, it is impossible to verify the precise details of Mrs. Doupe's ill bodings.

However, in tribute to her prophecy and to this strange journey with its yet unknown destination, Georgian Bay now has a Waubuno Channel and a Wreck Island.

An equally famous event, the loss of the schooner *Our*

Son,[2] is comparatively recent. It occurred on September 26, 1930. The disaster is particularly well documented partly because of a mistake in history. It is still thought by many to be the last commercial sailing vessel on the Great Lakes. But the reason it is included here is what historian Dwight Boyer called the "eerie chain of events that took place between dawn and midafternoon." What happened on Lake Michigan then "still defies rational and reasonable explanation," he wrote.

In 1930, the *Our Son*, a broken-down three-masted schooner, was 55 years old. She had a 73-year-old captain, Fred Nelson. On September 25, 1930, she was carrying pulpwood to the Central Paper Company in Muskegon, Mich. She would have arrived early the morning of September 26, had not a violent westerly gale of near hurricane strength slammed across Lake Michigan from one end to the other. The strong wind made quick work of all the schooner's canvas, leaving her without propulsion and consequently without any way of controlling her heading. Without control, the *Our Son* fell helplessly into the trough of the seas—the worst position with respect to the waves. The length of the *Our Son* was parallel to the waves and each new one rolled her mercilessly from side to side, washing over her and destroying everything above deck.

The waves were tremendous. Since the *Our Son* was on the western side of the lake, the seas had the full width of Lake Michigan to build before they crashed into the old wooden ship. The *Our Son* had no radios. It was dark. The ship was rapidly filling with water. She was far enough off any prescribed shipping lane so as to preclude hope of rescue. And the seas were violent enough to eliminate any possibility of launching a lifeboat. The storm showed no sign of subsiding. It was a serious situation. Facing death, the men of the *Our Son* could do nothing. They sat in the ship playing with pieces of rope. They picked putty out of the window sills. They watched the huge waves crash into the ship. And they eyed the 73-year-old Captain Nelson as he prayed for salvation from the inevitable.

Without editorializing on divinities or extrasensory

perception, suffice it to say that something quite strange was happening far to the north aboard the sturdy steamer *William Nelson*. Capt. Charles H. Mohr came into Lake Michigan through the Straits of Mackinac about dawn. He was intent on hugging the north shore until he could get around to the west side of the lake, where he planned to anchor on the lee side of Washington Island—a safe place to wait for the storm to abate. That was not so strange. What was strange was that Mohr did not do that. Historian Boyer describes what happened:

Against all the accepted rules of cautious seamanship, common sense, tradition and the procedures normally dictated by the existing weather conditions, he . . . [took] his ship down the east shore of Lake Michigan, the dreaded Manitou Passage. Once headed for Grays Reef and the "gut" between Middle Shoal and East Shoal, the seas building up the whole width of Lake Michigan began to punish the *William Nelson* unmercifully. They rose as high as the steering pole and swept her broadside with agonizing frequency. She rolled abominably, smothered with white water every few seconds. In the galley, dishes cascaded from their racks. The pans on the old coal range slid off the deck. In the firehold the men were hard put to keep their footing, let alone feed their boilers. Loose coal slid from side to side in miniature avalanches that swept up the slice bars and spare shovels. The crew must have been confounded by Capt. Mohr's decision. It just didn't make sense. Nevertheless, the *William Nelson* wallowed on down the fearful passage beyond Big Sable Point and Ludington, sustaining damage with every mile. Her afterhouse was jolted with every sea that came calling. Glass in the portholes was shattered. Watertight doors, even though "dogged down," were sprung. The bulkheads were bent in. Forward, the steel companionways between the Texas deck and the pilot house had been wrenched loose.

. . . [Capt. Mohr] once more altered course drastically hauling hard to starboard and steering directly west toward the far-distant Wisconsin shore. Butting into the huge seas that now assaulted her head to, the steamer suffered still more damage. Her fo'c'sle deck was pushed inward about six inches, bending the stanchions and beams. Then the pilot house windows were plucked out one by one, by the wind and seas boarding her over the bow. Capt. Mohr, still guided by that strange and subconscious force, kept her headed due west.

It was this unorthodox and dangerous course that took Mohr directly to the *Our Son*.

When Mohr saw the schooner, her flag flying upside down in distress, he used his radio to transmit a description of the situation. He circled the schooner pouring oil to reduce the severity of the waves. Then he nosed his ship up to the side of the schooner and the grateful sailors leaped helter-skelter for what must to them have seemed like the Rock of Gibraltar.

Odd—or reckless—as Captain Mohr's actions may seem, he was outdone in terms of stark implausibility by one Joseph A. Sadony, a self-proclaimed clairvoyant with a noteworthy record for predicting future events. More than two hours before the *William Nelson* first saw the *Our Son*, Sadony was standing outside near the east shore of Lake Michigan among a group of people. One of that group wondered aloud about ships that might be suffering upon the lake.

"There is one sailing ship to the northwest I would not want to be on," Sadony said.

Another member of the group helpfully, but erroneously, pointed out that there were no more sailing ships on the lakes.

Sadony nevertheless continued to describe just how the schooner was filling with water, how her sails were shredded, and how she was far off any normal course. He even said there was a steamer approaching the doomed schooner.

Add to the enormous improbability of these events Captain Mohr's history of similar rescues. Mohr saved seven from a sinking yacht in Georgian Bay in June 1922. In November 1926 he saved three from a disabled yacht in Lake Erie. In 1927 he rescued the crew of the *Mildred* during a Lake Erie snowstorm. And in July 1929 he rescued six after their yacht capsized in

Lake Erie. Even after a lifetime at sea, most mariners never come close to a single such disaster.

Milton Smith, assistant engineer of the steamer *Charles Price,*[3] followed his premonition and consequently lost his season's bonus. Crews like those on the *Charles Price* are paid, in addition to their salary, a bonus if they stay with their ship throughout the shipping season. This saves the company the personnel expense of hiring new people. Smith had only three weeks before he would have cashed in on his season's bonus, but he said frankly that he felt uneasy about continuing to sail on the *Price.* There was nothing wrong with the ship. Smith just felt uneasy.

Three days later, on November 12, 1913, the *Price* mysteriously sank. All hands were lost.

Just a few years before, at almost the same place the *Price* is believed to have disappeared, the *Aztec,*[4] under command of Capt. Dave Beggs, dropped anchor. Beggs had navigated the length of Lake Huron southward toward the St. Clair River through a fog so thick that much of the time he could not see his own ship outside the pilot house. His plan was to proceed southward on course until he heard the Lake Huron Lightship foghorn.

Captain Beggs never heard the Lake Huron Lightship that day. But something told Captain Beggs that he should not continue his voyage, so he dropped anchor. He couldn't be sure exactly where until the next day when the fog lifted. The *Aztec's* steering pole was tangled in the rigging of the lightship. Only a few more feet would have meant a collision. Unknown to anyone on the *Aztec,* the lightship's whistle was inoperative and had been so for several hours prior to Beggs' decision to drop anchor.

Capt. Bill Brian was skipper of the *Kamloops*[5] in 1927. His dog's name was Ginger. Ginger always accompanied Brian shipboard or ashore. At least she always accompanied him until December 1, 1927, about midnight. Captain Brian returned then to the *Kamloops,* but for no apparent reason Ginger refused to board the ship. She would not cross the gangplank. It was the first time she'd acted that way in the two years she'd been with Captain Brian. The men tried to catch her, but she eluded them. She would not board the ship. No one knew at the time what incredible events were about to overtake this ship and her crew. But Ginger's refusal to go aboard was the first strange aspect of this strange voyage. The unbelievable happened to the *Kamloops*. It happened the night of December 5. That story is in the next chapter.

Chapter Fifteen:

COMPLETE DISAPPEARANCES

There are thousands of ships and aircraft and men that have tried unsuccessfully to cross the Great Lakes. Their whereabouts are unknown.

The steamer *Kamloops*[1] sailed north before daylight on December 2, 1927, from Cortright, Ont., on the St. Clair River that connects Lake Huron with Lake Erie. Her destination was Ft. William, Ont., on Thunder Bay of Lake Superior.

At noon, December 3, she locked through the Soo and entered Lake Superior. The seas were heavy—not so heavy as to threaten the young *Kamloops*, which had weathered much worse, but heavy enough to endanger her primary cargo. That cargo was special, imported papermill machinery consigned to the Thunder Bay Paper Company. If the machinery was damaged it would be a year before the anxious company could receive the replacement shipment. To avoid the contingency, Capt. Bill Brian ordered his ship anchored on the lee side of Whitefish Point until the seas subsided.

The weather improving, the *Kamloops* weighed anchor late the afternoon of December 5. She pulled in behind the steamer *Quedoc*. The *Quedoc* was under command of Capt. Roy Simpson. The *Quedoc* had just locked through the Soo and headed upbound along the same northwesterly course that the *Kamloops* intended to follow. Although the seas were not threatening, they were enough to deserve consideration. The *Quedoc's* Captain Simpson noted that the ships that passed him downbound showed no sign of stress and he could see other ships steaming upbound ahead of him. The decision that Brian and Simpson each made was a safe one, made even safer by the presence of the other. When ships travel in pairs, help is always at hand should either encounter difficulty. The two ships traveling in tandem calculated the winds, the waves and their drift. They plotted their course along the normal route to Ft. William.

It is significant that the two captains considered all the known natural forces that affect a ship's course. During the night of December 6 and the day of December 7, something happened which neither captain had reckoned.

By late afternoon on December 7, both the *Kamloops* and the *Quedoc* were well to the south of their intended course. To this day it is uncertain how this happened, but subsequent developments overshadowed this question.

Since the *Quedoc* was directly ahead of the *Kamloops*, Captain Simpson was first to notice a problem facing the two ships. It was brought to his attention by the *Quedoc's* lookout, who until then had been quietly staring into the weather ahead, and who suddenly began frantically screaming to draw Captain Simpson's attention to the rocks ahead—rocks on which the *Quedoc* was about to destroy herself. Captain Simpson hurriedly ordered the wheelsman to turn to the right. In fact, he was screaming "Starboard, starboard," as he leaped for the wheel himself. The maneuver saved the *Quedoc*. And the narrow escape of the *Quedoc* would provide the men of the *Kamloops* with adequate warning of what was to come.

But the *Kamloops* didn't turn.

Captain Simpson began a series of short blasts on the *Quedoc's* steam whistle to warn the *Kamloops*, which was still steaming straight for the rocks.

The *Kamloops* sailed on.

That was the last anyone ever saw of the *Kamloops*.

Presumably, the *Kamloops* crashed into the rocks there on Isle Royale. But "presumably" doesn't mean much in this curious case.

There are at least two things that can happen to a steamer when it runs into a jagged shoreline like this one. The rocks can hold her there until the storm subsides. Or the waves can beat the ship to pieces, strewing the lake and shore with tons of wreckage. There may be another possibility. No one is sure what it is. But when this storm was over, this 2302-ton freighter was absent from the shore of Isle Royale. Nor was any trace left that she had ever been there.

This was extraordinary. Nothing. No *Kamloops*. No survivors. No bodies. No wreckage. No Captain Brian. And no papermill machinery. The only evidence that the *Kamloops* had ever existed was on paper. When a mysterious catastrophe occurs—especially if it promises to stay mysterious for several newspaper editions—reporters and editors can parlay the disaster into a bonanza. And this they did with the *Kamloops*. "Where is the *Kamloops*?" became the question of the day.

Two other company ships, the *Islet Prince* and the *Midland Prince,* began the search. The Canadian government sent a tug. The ship's owners chartered another tug. The U.S. Coast Guard cutter *Crawford* joined in. Coast Guardsmen and fishermen donned snowshoes and began a search of island shorelines. The ship's owners chartered an airplane.

All was futile.

Not so much as a lifejacket was ever found. There is no evidence even that the *Kamloops* sank.

To this day, there is nothing.

The *Inkerman*,[2] the *Cerisolles*[3] and the *Bautzen*[4] were built by a Canadian shipyard at Ft. William, Ont., for the French government. They were minesweepers—all identical. They left Ft. William the morning of November 24, 1918, headed for the Soo locks—the opposite course on which the *Kamloops* was to vanish nine years later. This trio was traveling together. Visibility diminished throughout November 24, so when the master of the *Bautzen* looked around and found the *Inkerman* and *Cerisolles* gone, he was not overly baffled. He continued on through the Soo on his journey to the Atlantic. The *Inkerman* and the *Cerisolles* never made it to the Soo. Presumably they are still somewhere in Lake Superior. They've not been seen since.

Subsequent search did not locate the two ships. In

fact, nary a scrap of wreckage was ever found to indicate that the two ships had ever existed. The French Navy crews likewise were lost. There were no survivors, no bodies, no evidence whatsoever.

The *D. M. Clemson*[5] was a 5531-ton steamer owned and operated by A. B. Wolvin of Duluth. She left Loraine, Ohio, on Lake Erie, the evening of November 29, 1908, loaded with coal. She passed into Lake Huron the next morning, November 30. At 9:30 A.M., on December 1, the *D. M. Clemson* passed through the Soo into Lake Superior. She was joined by another steamer, the *J. J. Brown*, which passed into Lake Superior with the *Clemson*.

Both were on the same upbound course intended by the *Kamloops*, opposite the downbound course of the *Inkerman*, *Cerisolles*, and, incidentally, the *Edmund Fitzgerald*. The *J. J. Brown* held to a more northerly heading than did the *D. M. Clemson*. The crew of the *J. J. Brown* watched the *D. M. Clemson* fade into the distance. No one has ever seen the *D. M. Clemson* since. Historian Dwight Boyer describes various attempts to resolve the phenomenon:

> Many shipmasters were of the opinion that she had suffered a serious mechanical breakdown and while without power to help herself, fell into the trough of overwhelming seas. But surely, in such an event would it not take several such seas to engulf her? They would almost certainly have swept her decks clear of cabins and pilothouse, littering the seas with her wooden paneling, furniture, bodies, trunks, hatchcovers, mattresses and other debris. With so many vessels searching and watching, something would have been found to indicate that the ship had been pounded to pieces by the seas.
>
> Others hinted that in the gale (a week before) the *Clemson* had encountered on her downbound trip she may have suffered severe structural damage, damage that went undetected until the wrenching and twisting of the second storm caused her to fracture plates and open her hull to the seas. But Capt. Sam Chamberlain had inspected his ship that Thanksgiving Day morning and found not so much as a sheared rivet!

The thorough search for the *D. M. Clemson* or some evidence of what could have happened to her was continued right up until the winter freeze. Nothing was found.

There is a plausible explanation for the loss of the *Benjamin Noble*[6] in 1914. Investigation subsequent to the disappearance of the 1481-ton steamer showed she was grossly overloaded and trying to make her way through a terrible gale into Duluth, Minn., at night while one of the lights marking the harbor entrance was extinguished. It would be reasonable to expect the five-year-old ship to sink. But if she sank, where is she? No bodies and no wreck have ever been discovered. The *Benjamin Noble* has not been seen since that night.

The *Inkerman*, the *Cerisolles*, the *Fitzgerald*, the *Bannockburn*, and several others all have disappeared within the southeastern corner of Lake Superior between Whitefish Point and Keweenaw Point. Why so many of the strange accidents of Lake Superior should occur in the confines of this small section of the lake remains a mystery. But this precedent set by shipping has been paralleled by the same kind of concentration of aircraft disappearances over this one small part of Lake Superior.

Wayne Robertson, for example, left Ann Arbor, Mich., not far from Detroit, on May 29, 1970. It was a fairly long trip in a Cessna 172 like N7487T[7] to Ontonagon, Mich. Ontonagon is on the west side of Keweenaw Point. So, on the return trip on May 30, Robertson came east across the point and then across the waters of southeast Lake Superior where so many others before him had vanished. Robertson vanished. That was sometime after 11:30 A.M., on May 31. Nothing has ever been seen since of Robertson or the Cessna 172 in which he attempted the flight.

About 11:45 A.M. on November 28, 1952, F. Jake left Houghton, Mich., on Keweenaw Point in a Beech

35, Canadian registration CF-FUV,[8] headed southeast for Toronto, Ont. U.S. radar stations watched him proceed across these strange waters between Keweenaw Point and Whitefish Point. They watched him proceed until target CF-FUV disappeared. In such cases, it is a simple matter for a radar controller to direct search and rescue aircraft to the accident site, by directing those targets to where the target disappeared. If CF-FUV did crash, then something else very strange happened to it.

As the Canadian accident report explained it, "despite an extensive search, no trace of the aircraft or occupants was found."

The official reason for CF-FUV's loss is "undetermined."

The same dilemma faced the Coast Guard and the Civil Air Patrol after the crash on December 19, 1966, of N2347U,[9] a Cessna 172 piloted by Anthony R. Farinacci. It disappeared over the southern shore of Lake Erie near Ashtabula, Ohio. N2347U had reported peculiar problems and Cleveland Center was watching it carefully when it vanished. More than a dozen airplanes, helicopters and Coast Guard cutters converged for the search, which lasted for five days. Not a body, not a scrap of wreckage, nothing was ever recovered.

In southern Lake Michigan east of a line between Chicago and Milwaukee, there is another area into which ships and airplanes frequently disappear.

On November 6, 1969, at 8:07 A.M., a twin turbojet aircraft, Lear model 23A, owned and operated by Mack Trucks, Inc., left its homebase in Allentown, Pa., for a corporate business flight to Horlick-Racine Airport, Racine, Wisc., to meet with a radiator manufacturer. At the controls were two highly qualified professional pilots, James R. Simmons in command and George K. Strunk flying as copilot. Together, they had almost 10,000 hours' experience. They carried five passengers.

As they neared Lake Michigan, they were on the identical course flown by United 389 five years earlier. But this particular Lear Jet, Lear N1021B,[10] altered its planned course just as it reached the eastern shore of Lake Michigan westbound. Because of thick fog reported in the Racine area, N1021B turned southward to land at Benton Harbor and wait out the weather—a responsible action that a less careful pilot might have foregone.

At 12:44 P.M., Racine time, N1021B departed Benton Harbor on the eastern shore of Lake Michigan. It was headed across the lake. At 1:01 P.M., just after N1021B crossed the point at which United 389 had been cleared down to 6000 feet, N1021B itself was cleared down to 6000 feet, and handed off to Milwaukee Approach Control. Milwaukee handled the approaches going into Horlick-Racine Airport, which is about 15 miles south of Milwaukee. The Milwaukee Approach controller handling the flight began giving N1021B directions for an approach into Milwaukee, but the alert pilots quickly corrected the controller. Racine was their intended destination.

At 1:05 P.M., N1021B intercepted the final approach course into Horlick-Racine Airport. The jet was still over Lake Michigan, approaching the airport from the east. At 1:07 P.M., Milwaukee Approach, monitoring the flight on radar, told N1021B that it was four miles from the airport, still over Lake Michigan. N1021B was slightly left of course—well within normal limits.

Ten seconds later Milwaukee radar was no longer receiving an echo from N1021B, nor was it receiving a reply from N1021B's transponder. Electronically, at least, N1021B no longer existed.

Later Lee L. Hansen told authorities that at about that time, "we were standing on the beach just down from the church when we heard a loud roar that lasted about ten seconds. It came from the northeast over the lake."

Emery L. Kreuziger said, "It sounded like a motor boat, yet it sounded like an airplane. So I went to the lake to see what was coming. All of a sudden I heard a noise like two bangs—pop, pop—and then silence."

The investigators never found anyone who actually saw N1021B. They never found N1021B. None of the seven bodies has been recovered. The search was extensive. The probable cause of the occurrence is "undetermined."

Anderson Duggar, Jr., was alone in his twin Piper PA-31, registration N212AD,[11] on July 21, 1972. He left Detroit en route to Milwaukee on business. His flight path took him over the same waters where so many have disappeared. He was an experienced pilot with more than 4000 hours at the controls. Weather was excellent at Milwaukee. Duggar was in radio contact with Milwaukee Approach Control. No sign of trouble was indicated in the radio conversations with N212AD. Milwaukee Approach was watching Duggar on radar. Duggar was about 15 miles east of Milwaukee over Lake Michigan. He was at an enroute altitude a mile above the lake surface westbound as expected. That was 9:10 A.M.

That was the moment when Duggar and N212AD flew out of existence. Milwaukee Approach radar stopped painting a target for Duggar. The controller could no longer contact Duggar on radio. And no one has ever seen Duggar since. No wreckage was found. No bodies were found. The search was extensive.

Despite Milwaukee Approach's efforts to direct rescue craft directly to the point of disappearance on this clear morning, not a scrap of wreckage was found. The face of Lake Michigan displayed not a trace of anything unusual. The report of the accident begins, "It is presumed that the aircraft crashed into Lake Michigan 15 miles east of Milwaukee, Wisc., and that the pilot received fatal injuries." The presumption is questionable. The cause of the occurrence is "undetermined."

At 6:01 P.M., on December 7, 1972, James Rose, 47, left Moline, Ill., in N9002G[12] on a return flight to Northbrook, Ill., just north of Chicago on the west shore of Lake Michigan. He was an experienced private pilot who had flown for 13 years. He had been checked out by an instructor pilot only four days before. The instructor tested Rose's ability to plan and conduct a cross-country flight. No problems were noted on the checkout.

Yet, at 8:20 P.M. on December 7, Rose was far off

course to the north talking to Milwaukee Radio. He was near Janesville. Milwaukee Radio had Rose read off a number of radials as indicated on Rose's navigational radios, from various navigational transmitters in the area. Based on that information, Milwaukee Radio gave Rose a course that would take him directly to his intended destination, Northbrook.

There was something strange about Rose's request, and Milwaukee Radio was concerned about the flight. So the communicator asked Rose to confirm each detail of the instructions. Based on these communications, it is known that Rose must have been on course with his navigation radios set properly. He was flying toward Northbrook. According to his position and direction information, Rose was well within range for radio communication with Chicago Radio. But he couldn't make contact. Milwaukee Radio heard him trying. Milwaukee Radio even heard him fade away as he got closer and closer to Chicago.

The Milwaukee Radio communicators were worried, so they teletyped Chicago Radio advising them of the situation. Chicago Radio never heard Rose. In fact, no one has ever heard from him. The Civil Air Patrol looked. They searched diligently. But they failed. Some aircraft parts did wash ashore near Milwaukee. Investigators guessed that the parts might be from Rose's airplane. While these parts are consistent with wreckage that would be expected from the plane Rose was flying, the location of the parts near Milwaukee is at odds with the fact that to Milwaukee Radio, Rose's signal was getting weaker and weaker until it faded away. The location of the parts indicates Rose was flying toward this dangerous area of Lake Michigan where so many others have vanished.

But how could Rose—flying in visual conditions as he was—possibly have flown out over Lake Michigan without realizing that he *had* to have been flying away from his destination?

Under the circumstances the National Transport Safety Board could not assign a cause to the accident. In fact, the very conclusion that Rose crashed and died can only be "presumed."

Even for a man of 50, Lawrence Nelms was a highly experienced pilot, with more than 21,000 hours in the air. The night of November 30, 1972, Nelms was at the controls of a large Beech Expeditor 3TM carrying cargo from Detroit to Milwaukee, squarely through this block of deadly airspace. The day before, Nelms had passed his rigid "six-month check," which is required only of pilots who fly commercially through bad weather. The weather on November 30, however, was not bad—and for a man of Nelms' experience it was a beautiful day. Even if the weather had been bad, it would have made little difference. N15212,[13] the sturdy Expeditor that Nelms was flying, had been equipped for every contingency. But since the weather was good, Nelms did not file for an instrument clearance. This means that Air Traffic Control was not following N15212. Detroit Metropolitan Airport Tower simply cleared N15212 for takeoff at 9:23 P.M. N15212 turned westward toward Lake Michigan. Its estimated time of arrival was 10:05 P.M. Milwaukee.

N15212 disappeared.

Despite the diligent efforts of the Coast Guard and the Civil Air Patrol, there is today no physical evidence that either Nelms or N15212 ever existed. Not so much as a scrap of wreckage was found. Like Anderson Duggar, Jr., who disappeared while trying to fly the same route four months earlier on July 21, Nelms never transmitted a distress call. Whatever obliterated N15212 did so quickly.

One of the most publicized disappearances of this region was the "Mystery of the Vanishing Aviatrix." She was Miss Joan Williams, 39, a Chicago Heights schoolteacher, who owned a Cessna 170B, N2522C.[14] She left Wings Airport, Chicago, at noon on a Saturday morning, March 20, 1965, carrying fuel sufficient for four hours, 30 minutes. She was not on a flight plan. She has not been seen since.

For some reason the case stimulated the interest of the Chicago newspapers. It stayed in the headlines for weeks as officials searched vainly for some evidence of what happened. Virtually everyone Miss Williams knew was contacted. Her bank records and personal life were investigated thoroughly on the chance that the disappearance was intentional. The lake was combed for some scrap of wreckage that would solve the mystery.

It has been more than ten years. Government files show no evidence of what could have become of Miss Williams or N2522C.

William A. Sells, 38, a Civil Air Patrol pilot, was called on to help with search and rescue operations out of Muskegon, Mich., on January 14, 1967. Another airplane was overdue and presumed crashed. So Sells in N9201A[15] and his passengers, Mrs. Eva Howse and Rodney Lewis, left Benton Harbor, Mich., at 11:45 A.M. northbound along the eastern shoreline of Lake Michigan to Muskegon. That short flight was almost entirely within the area in which Northwest Airlines Flight 2501 is believed to have vanished. The disappearance of Northwest 2501 in 1950 has remained a mystery to this day. The Civil Air Patrol was hoping for better luck on March 20, 1965.

Instead, Sells disappeared—as did his two passengers and his airplane.

The Civil Air Patrol was faced with the embarrassing business of looking for its own airplane. The Civil Air Patrol's failure in that endeavor was even more embarrassing. To this day no one knows what became of N9201A.

It was a perfect, clear day on May 21, 1969, in Michigan when Richard B. Dotson, Manley V. Meddaugh, Jack Ressequie and Jean Ressequie were returning to Lansing from a trip to Negaunee. Dotson and Meddaugh were the pilots on the Beech 35, registration N3358V.[16] Since pilots who fly the Great Lakes know of the strange dangers there, Dotson and Meddaugh were expected to go out of their way by crossing Lake Michigan at the Straits of Mackinac. This would have kept them almost continuously over land.

But Dotson and Meddaugh chose a more direct, southerly route. N3358V was on a visual flight plan when at 2:35 P.M., May 21, 1969, one of the pilots reported their position at Menominee, Mich. Menominee is on the northwest shore of Lake Michigan and N3358V was southeastbound across the lake at 7500 feet. This meant that if N3358V suffered total power failure it would have had more than ten minutes to initiate a distress call before gliding below the altitude at which a call might go unheard. Except for about 15 minutes of the flight, it would all be within gliding distance of land. In any case the 2:35 P.M. position report was the last anyone heard of N3358V. Dotson and Meddaugh never radioed for help, and they never made it to Lansing. All four occupants are "presumed" dead, though no bodies have been found. The cause of this presumed crash has remained "undetermined."

Lawrence J. Fayton, his wife, Judith, and their children, Jennifer, Bradley, Rebecca, Brian and Lawrence, left Ithaca, N.Y., in Cessna 172, N8443X,[17] on a return trip to their home near Detroit, Mich. Mr. Fayton was at the controls. At 5:33 P.M., he reported he was over Lake Erie on course about halfway from Dunkirk, N.Y., to Long Point, Ont. Fayton estimated his time of arrival at Long Point at 5:45 P.M. He never reported any trouble. He never reported reaching Long Point.

The National Transportation Safety Board chose not to venture a guess as to what might have ended this flight. But there are certain facts available. A Cessna 172 travels only about 24 miles in 12 minutes, like the 12 minutes during which Fayton and his family vanished. That is a comparatively small area in which to find an airplane and seven human beings, when they are the only ones there. But no member of the Fayton family has been found. Neither has N8443X.

Civil Air Patrol airplanes, Coast Guard helicopters and airplanes, Canadian Air Force aircraft, Coast Guard buoy tenders and Coast Guard motor lifeboats all combed the area in a search that eventually covered much of Lake Erie as well as the New York and Pennsylvania shorelines for a number of miles inland. Nevertheless, as of February the following year, "no trace of the aircraft or its occupants has been found," wrote Daniel C. Sayres, Air Safety Investigator. How is that possible? Sayres did not say. Fayton was an inexperienced pilot. That may have led to an accident, but it doesn't explain his vanishing from the face of the earth.

William P. Finney, on the other hand, had a great deal of experience—more than 22,000 hours, in fact. He was an airline transport pilot and on March 20, 1973, he was flying a Beech F18S, registration N1900R,[18] on a cargo flight out of Cleveland. Like Fayton before him, Finney was headed for Detroit.

Like Fayton before him, Finney vanished.

Finney took off at 11:15 P.M. It was a 45-minute trip. Six hours later the Coast Guard was covering the same route. Two days later, they were covering all of western Lake Erie. Still, according to the National Transportation Safety Board, no one has heard or seen Finney or N1900R since it left Cleveland. The airplane is presumed destroyed and Finney is presumed dead.

One of the most extraordinary disappearances occurred the night of April 20, 1973, somewhere over Lake Erie between Erie, Pa., and Howell, Mich.[19] Robert Joy, Jr., 30, alone at the controls of his light Citabria landplane, and his father Robert Joy, 51, alone at the controls of his Lake seaplane, left Erie in formation. The Lake is a faster airplane than the Citabria, so Joy Sr. slowed it down to stay behind his son.

Theirs was an excellent plan for safely ferrying a landplane over water. If anything happens to force the landplane to ditch (ditching is when a landplane lands on water), the seaplane can follow it down and rescue the occupants before they get their feet wet. Alternatively, if the seaplane experiences a problem, it can land while the landplane circles above. If the seaplane's problems cannot be corrected, the landplane can direct rescuers to the downed seaplane.

At 10:45 P.M., on April 20, both the Citabria and

the Lake were nearing the north shore of Lake Erie. There were no problems. The senior Joy was tired of following his slower son. So he radioed that he would proceed on ahead and meet his son at their destination, Howell, in about 20 minutes. This was not dangerous. At worst, if the Citabria developed a problem, the younger Joy could radio his father and the seaplane could quickly return. They would never be out of radio contact with each other, and if the Citabria ditched, it would float for hours, perhaps even days.

Just before 11:00 P.M. the younger Joy arrived in Howell. He was surprised that his father was not there to meet him. He checked further. His father had not landed. The next day, his father still had not landed. Joy Jr. was not alarmed, though. He told *The Cleveland Plain Dealer* that his father was an excellent pilot capable of handling any emergency that could have arisen under the circumstances. Waves on the lake that night were only one to two feet, and the Lake seaplane that the senior Joy was flying could easily ride out four-foot seas.

The combined efforts of the Coast Guard, the Michigan Civil Air Patrol and the Canadian Mounted Police confirmed the next day that the elder Joy and his seaplane were not on the face of Lake Erie.

The search continued long after there was any hope of finding Joy alive. In the interest of future aviation safety it was important to learn what swallowed the seaplane and its pilot. Not a scrap of evidence was ever found. Nothing has been seen of the senior Joy's seaplane since his son watched its navigation lights fade into the darkness ahead.

This flight was over the same part of Lake Erie that would have been traveled by the schooner *South America*.[20] Historian Mansfield wrote in 1899:

The schooner *South America*, Capt. Brady, left Buffalo, November 4 [1843], with a cargo of salt for Toledo, and was never heard of afterwards. This was the most deplorable disaster of the season; six lives lost.

The same thing happened to the new schooner *Kate Norton*[21] in Lake Erie. Historian Thomas Bowen writes:

Most of the Milan-built boats had long and successful careers. However, one, the *Kate Norton*, had a very short existence and a tragic ending. Proclaimed as one of the smartest vessels to be launched in the late 1850's, she was outfitted for the Great Lakes trade and left Milan late one Friday afternoon in the Spring, with her white sails bellying to the breeze, and her fresh paint and varnish work glistening in the setting sun. Thus did the schooner *Kate Norton*, under the command of Capt. Homer Beardsley, clear the harbor of Huron and enter Lake Erie. She sailed away into eternity. Her first night on the "great waters" was also her last, a rare record for a sturdy ship.

Almost directly over the spot where the *Jane Miller* (see Chapter Five) vanished in 1881, a twin-engine Piper PA-30, registration N7659Y,[22] made its last position report at 2:30 A.M., on March 17, 1966.

Ernest Eugene Nabors, 48, a highly qualified professional pilot working for Alpena Flying Service, Inc., departed Phelps Collins Airport, Alpena, Mich., at 4:38 P.M., March 16, 1966. His destination was Bradley Field, Windsor Locks, Conn. The sky was clear and visibility was unrestricted all along this route, and the night was forecast to remain so.

Nabors made the flight for the Alpena Paper Company, which needed 450 pounds of liquid chemicals from the Monsanto Chemical Co. N7659Y arrived at Windsor Locks at 7:52 P.M., ahead of schedule. He unloaded the chemicals and departed at 9:59 P.M. At midnight, N7659Y reported over Albany, N.Y. The time of the report was very curious. It meant that Nabors had taken two hours to fly what should have been a 30-minute leg. This mystery was solved a few months later, when Nabors' wife produced a fuel bill that showed Nabors had flown to Westerly, R.I., and refueled before beginning his trip home.

At 2:30 A.M. on March 17, N7659Y reported over

Wiarton, Ont., on course to his homebase with everything proceeding smoothly. He told the Wiarton Department of Transport Communications Station that his estimated time of arrival back at homebase, Alpena, Mich., was 3:20 A.M.—50 minutes away.

The Civil Aeronautics Board reported six months later that "an extensive search by U.S. and Canadian Air/Sea Rescue Services has failed to locate the aircraft or pilot."

At first the Civil Aeronautics Board investigators calculated that Nabors had run N7659Y out of fuel over Lake Huron between his last position report, Wiarton, and his destination, Alpena. This would have made sense if N7659Y had been in the air continuously since leaving Albany. But Nabors' friends knew he was too good a pilot to make a mistake like that.

"I strongly urge that your office continue an extensive search in the area between Windsor Locks and Albany in an attempt to find the missing time," wrote Nabors' employer. The missing time was the difference between the 30 minutes that the leg should have taken and the two hours it actually took. The missing fuel ticket, found by Nabors' widow, resolved the question, thereby invalidating the only plausible explanation for Nabors' disappearance.

The search lasted for weeks. No evidence of a crash or a ditching on Lake Huron was discovered. Nabors' body has never been recovered.

Two CF-101 Canadian Air Force twin-jet interceptors were in a night formation close to where pilot Nabors made his last position report. The leader of that night formation of interceptors recalls that the number two plane's pilot complained of "vertigo." The number two interceptor then vanished. Despite the leader's noting the exact location of this strange occurrence, neither the aircraft nor its occupants have been found.[23]

Another formation of Canadian interceptors was flying over Lake Ontario on September 27, 1960, on a clear day, when the number two jet's pilot looked up from his instruments and noticed that the number one jet, No.

18469,[24] was no longer ahead of him. The first interceptor's contrail just ended in midair. There was no distress call. The number one jet has never been found. (See Chapter Five)

Some of the strangest disappearances in this area don't involve either aircraft or ships. About 45 miles north of Lake Ontario, scientists are studying the disappearance of huge chunks of earth which have mysteriously been cut from the ground and removed.

Local authorities believe the mysterious occurrences are related to a number of close-up UFO encounters nearby. Reports show that the large chunks of sod have been carved out of meadows. The land around the holes shows no evidence that any kind of heavy machinery was driven into the area. On some occasions, the chunks of earth have been found some distance away, unbroken— still in the shape of the hole from which they were removed. The phenomenon has caused some concern among local residents, many of whom have heard strange beeping sounds coming from the meadows and pastures at night near their homes.[25]

Pilot Maurice J. Merickel and passenger S. Niesses left Sioux Narrows on May 21, 1959, in a Piper PA-18, registration N9081D.[26] The plan was to fly the seaplane to an unnamed lake, pick up a canoe, tie it to the pontoons of the seaplane and then fly to Teggau Lake, Ont., northwest of Lake Superior. The canoe was found in Teggau Lake with impact damage. Any number of things might have happened to N9081D, but the subsequent search for the aircraft and its two occupants proved bizarre. The Canada Department of Transport report reads as follows:

> An extensive search of the lake was made by dragging, use of underwater detection equipment, divers, deep sea bell and sonar equipment. Several sweeps were also made with airborne detection equipment. Grappling hooks engaged an object where detection gear had given a strong reading, but all efforts to bring the object to the surface failed. The object engaged was in 320 feet of

water. A diver descended to 250 feet but due to darkness under water could not make any visual contact. The sonar gear established that the lake bottom was very uneven with deep holes, the deepest being 590 feet. The operation was discontinued on July 6, 1959.

N9081D was never found. The strange object that was found has never been identified.

These are just a few of the examples of aircraft and ships that have perished in the Great Lakes region. In each case, their whereabouts are unknown.

Chapter Sixteen:

THE BODIES

Many of the unexplainable events of the Great Lakes involve strange disposition of the bodies of those involved.

At midnight, the night of December 16, 1959, pilots Jack Stewart Murphy and Peter Francis Colontino were making their approach into the Windsor, Ont., airport, across the Detroit River from Detroit, Mich. They were flying an Aero Design 560E, registration CF-KDW.[1] No difficulty was reported. There was no hint of panic or confusion in the pilot's voice. CF-KDW acknowledged Air Traffic Control instructions to report five miles from the runway. The report was never made. The following morning debris from CF-KDW was floating on Lake St. Clair. Six days later the badly damaged aircraft was raised to the surface. It was evident that impact was tremendous. Accident investigators were concerned only with the cause of the accident. The cause was unexplainable.

But a bigger mystery involved the bodies of Murphy and Colontino. The impact clearly was not survivable, yet the two were not in the airplane. Their bodies have not been found.

The same was true in the famous *Waubuno* disaster of 1879, which has been discussed in Chapter Fourteen. It was the strange catastrophe foretold by Mrs. W. D. Doupe's vision. The passenger steamer, still afloat, was found badly battered. There were no bodies in it. No bodies were ever recovered, despite the recovery of every single lifejackets aboard.

However, bodies were recovered from the *Regina*,[2] the

173

James C. Carruthers[3] and the *Charles Price*.[4] But in these curious cases, the bodies raised more questions than they answered. All three ships were lost in the great gale of November 11, 1913.

The *James C. Carruthers* was Canada's largest and newest grain carrier, 550 feet long and 5606 tons. She was carrying 340,000 bushels of wheat and a crew of 19. She was downbound in Lake Huron on a voyage that had begun in Ft. William, Ont., on the north shore of Lake Superior.

The huge 10,000-ton *Charles Price* has already been discussed because of assistant engineer Milton Smith's vision of impending doom. (See Chapter Fourteen) The *Price* was just into Lake Huron northbound from Ashtabula, Ohio, on Lake Erie to Superior, Wisc., at the western tip of Lake Superior. The *Charles Price's* cargo was 9000 tons of soft coal. All hands were lost but the ship floated for days.

The *Regina* was a 269-foot Canadian package freighter She was a steamer of 1956 tons, carrying mostly lumber. She was lost without a trace.

Through the weeks following, bodies from all three ships floated ashore. Many historians have studied the eerie circumstances involving these bodies. William Ratigan recorded what happened with identification of one of the first bodies:

> The first body he was asked to identify gave him a shock. Despite the ruthless battering of the storm, he recognized his former chief, John Groundwater.
>
> "That's big good-natured John," he said. "All the boys like him."
>
> "Are you sure?" demanded the coroner.
>
> "Sure I'm sure. I worked under him all season. I saw him just last Saturday. I ought to know. Why? What's the trouble?"
>
> "If he was chief engineer aboard the *Price*," said the coroner, "then why has he got a *Regina* life preserver wrapped around him?"

The question has echoed from 1913 to this day. Other bodies identified as from the crew of the *Price* were picked up also wearing life preservers marked *Regina*. It may be speculated that the two boats were slammed together in the storm so that men passed from one deck to the other, seizing any life preserver handy. Perhaps as the ships were sinking, life preservers thrown to those knocked into the water by the theoretical collision were grabbed at by members of both crews struggling to stay afloat.

Historian Dwight Boyer studied the case and described the same scene as "the only explanation that made sense."

Unfortunately this "only explanation that made sense" later turned out to be inconsistent with the facts of the case.

"When last sighted, and apparently not long before they went down, the two vessels were at least 15 miles apart," wrote Boyer. Actually, this is conservative. The two were probably a good deal more than 15 miles apart.

But even more devastating to the collision theory was evidence found when divers examined the still-floating hull of the *Charles Price*. What they found is as follows:

There was no other vessel under the bow of the *Price*; the diver found that the buoyancy of the hull was due to imprisoned air, now slowly escaping in two streams of bubbles. Careful investigating revealed not a sign of any collision and so the mystery of why *Price* men had been washed ashore wearing *Regina* life preservers was deeper than ever.

Like Milton Smith, who had quit the *Price* before her last voyage, John Thompson quit the *James Carruthers* just in time to avoid dying on her. According to Thompson, anyway, he did not die on the ship. A dead body, greatly resembling Thompson, did wash ashore. The resemblance was remarkable. Both the living John Thompson and the dead man had the initials "J.T." tattooed on the left forearm. They had the same scars on the nose and leg. They had the same dental peculiarities. And each had the same two deformed toes. Beyond that, John Thompson's father at first identified the dead man as his son. Other members of the family agreed with the father's judgment. When the living version of John Thompson finally showed up at his own wake, he convinced his family who he was and thereby scotched the rumors of his demise.

This mystery has not been solved.

While history recorded too many John Thompsons, the world is still short one George R. Donner. Donner was skipper of the *O. M. McFarland*,[5] carrying 5800 tons of coal from Erie, Pa., on Lake Erie to Port Washington, Wisc., on Lake Michigan just north of Milwaukee. At 10:15 P.M., on April 28, 1937, he left the pilot house to get some rest in his cabin. The weather was good. He left word to be awakened when the ship was in sight of her destination. Donner was later heard moving around in his cabin. At 1:15 A.M., as the *McFarland* neared Port Washington, the mate knocked on the cabin door. A few minutes later, the second officer opened the door. Donner was not there. A subsequent search of the ship verified his complete absence. The next day *The Cleveland Press* reported the following:

> A new mystery of the Great Lakes was unfolded today when the freighter *O. S. McFarland* [sic] docked at Pt. Washington, Wisc., and crew members reported the disappearance of the ship's master.

It is quite unlikely that an experienced seaman like Donner would fall overboard in calm seas. Besides, Donner had gone to his room to get sleep. There is no plausible reason for him to be anywhere that any person could fall overboard. But, in any case, no body was ever found. Donner's whereabouts are still unknown.

Historian Mansfield recorded an even stranger disposition of a body aboard the *New Connecticut*[6] in 1833:

> In the Autumn of 1833, Capt. Gilman Appleby, of Conneaut, Ohio, was captain and part owner of the schooner *New Connecticut*. A steamboat was then being built at Conneaut (the *North American*) of which Capt. Appleby had charge and was for many years her master. An aunt of his then residing at Black Rock, below Buffalo, was visiting a brother at Erie. The lady

went to Conneaut in company with a nephew to visit a brother there. After remaining there some time she became exceedingly anxious to get home. Capt. Appleby, who was busy with the steamboat, endeavored to dissuade her from taking the home journey until he should be going out with his vessel, when he would take her home. His efforts, however, in that direction were unavailing, and he had her taken on board the schooner to go to Buffalo in charge of the crew. Everything passed off quietly until after the vessel passed Erie, when a sudden squall struck her and rolled her over on her side. She nearly filled with water but continued to float. The crew, lowering the vessel's yawl, jumped in and pulled for the shore, leaving the woman in the cabin, as they supposed, drowned. The party landed at or near Portland, Chautauqua Co., N.Y., and made their way as best they could back to Conneaut.

Three days after the accident, Capt. Wilkins, of the steamboat *William Peacock*, in coming down from Detroit, was besought by Capt. Appleby to board the wreck if he saw it, and if possible get the body of his aunt out of the cabin and convey it to Buffalo. Capt. Wilkins discovered the disabled vessel drifting down the lake, and after coming alongside, Capt. William Henton (then first mate of the *Peacock*) boarded the wreck and made search. The schooner lay upon her side, and to all appearances, was full of water. A pole was employed, and it was supposed every part of the cabin was touched, and as no object in the shape of a human body was reached, the conclusion was, that the body had floated out of the cabin into the lake; hence further search was given up. Two days afterward, Capt. Appleby came down with a vessel with facilities to right the schooner and tow her to the nearest port.

When the vessel had nearly reached a level position, the woman walked through the water and came up the stairs to the deck. She was caught by Capt. Appleby and supported, while her son, who was present, wept and the sailors screamed.

177

EPILOGUE

In the course of researching and writing this book, many have asked what *really* caused the events herein described.

I do not *know*.

NOTES

To avoid repetition, all sources for each accident are combined into one note for that accident, except where confusion may result. The note is designated in the text next to the vessel name or aircraft call sign.

For brevity, names of government agencies and instructions on how to obtain source material are not repeated in each chapter. After first reference, subsequent references throughout all chapters are abbreviated.

Chapter One

1. Civil Aeronautics Board (CAB), "Accident Investigation Report," docket 1-0081 (requests for all U.S. civil aviation accident reports cited hereafter should be addressed to the National Transportation Safety Board, Washington, D.C., and should include aircraft registration number; date or presumed date of accident; and accident place, presumed accident place or place of departure); *Chicago Tribune*, June 25, 1950; idem, June 26, 1950; idem, June 27, 1950.

2. U.S. Coast Guard, "Background Information on SS *Edmund Fitzgerald*, lost on Lake Superior 10 November 1975," released by Department of Public Affairs by direction of Commander, Ninth Coast Guard District, 1240 East 9th St., Cleveland, Ohio 44199; U.S. Coast Guard, transcript of testimony by Capt. Jesse B. Cooper to Marine Board of Investigation into loss of SS *Edmund Fitzgerald*, available by request to Marine Board of Investigation Chairman RADM. Winford W. Barrow, Commander, Eighth Coast Guard District, New Orleans, La.

3. Originally this conclusion was based on three computer searches conducted at the author's request by the National Transportation Safety Board (NTSB). They are: "Listing of Missing Aircraft, Not Recovered, U.S. Civil Aviation, 1964-1975 (75 Incomplete)"; "Briefs of Accidents Where Cause Is Undetermined, States Bordering Great Lakes, and Canada, U.S. Civil Aviation, 1964-1975 (75 Incomplete)"; and "Listing of Accidents Where Cause Is Undetermined, U.S. Civil Aviation, 1964-1975 (75 Incomplete)."

Chapter Two

1. William H. Allen and Harold A. Jacobs, CAB, "Factual Report of Investigation," docket 2-0977; CAB, "Accident Briefs—

U.S. General Aviation," docket 2-0977; CAB, "Analysis Report of Investigator-in-charge." (The last document is confidential. It should be requested as described in note 1, Chapter One. In addition the request should be made under the Freedom of Information Act, and this book should be cited as evidence that the secrecy of the document is no longer protectable. Such documents will be designated hereafter with the word "confidential.")

2. Canada Department of Transport, Air Services, Civil Aviation Branch, "Accident Report," serial 1909. (Requests for all Canadian civil-aviation accident reports cited hereafter should be addressed to Transport Canada Air, Ottawa, Ont., and should include aircraft registration number; date or presumed date of accident; and accident place, presumed accident place or place of departure.)

3. Dwight Boyer, *Ghost Ships of the Great Lakes* (New York: Dodd, Mead & Company, 1968) pp. 14-27; William Ratigan, *Great Lakes Shipwrecks & Survivals* (New York: Galahad Books, 1960) p. 270; *Chicago Tribune*, Nov. 28, 1902; personal letter no. 1600-6 (CCGH), Jan. 7, 1976, from Thomas E. Appleton, Canadian Coast Guard Historian, Transport Canada Marine, Ottawa, Ont., to Jay Gourley, author.

4. J. O. Johnson, NTSB, "Factual," CHI 73-A-C006; NTSB, "Briefs," file 3-1082.

5. The relevant documents were classified top secret. Certain information from them will be made available on personal request to the Directorate of Information Services, National Defence Headquarters, 101 Colonel By Drive, Ottawa, Ont. Request should include type of aircraft, registration number and date of occurrence. This book should be cited to show that the secrecy of the document is no longer protectable.

6. J. O. Johnson, NTSB, "Factual," CHI 73-A-C058; NTSB, "Briefs," file 3-4099; E. B. Kraus, NTSB, "Group Chairman's Factual Report of Investigation: Systems and Structures," CHI 73-A-C058 (confidential); John G. Young, NTSB, "Powerplant Investigator's Factual Report of Investigation," CHI 73-A-C058 (confidential); Reese C. Zantop, chief pilot, Zantop Airways, Detroit Metropolitan Airport, "Pilot/Operator Aircraft Accident Report," CHI 73-A-C058.

7. CAB, "Briefs," docket 2-4466.

8. Dwight Boyer, *Great Stories of the Great Lakes* (New York: Dodd, Mead & Company, 1966) pp. 60-8; John Brandt Mansfield, ed. and comp., *History of the Great Lakes* (Chicago: J. H. Beers & Co., 1899), p. 763; *Chicago Tribune*, Nov. 2, 1892.

9. Canada, Air Services, "Accident Report," serial 52-51.

10. Dwight Boyer, *Strange Adventures of the Great Lakes* (New York: Dodd, Mead & Company, 1974) p. 64; U.S. Life Saving Service, *Annual Report of 1900*, "Services of Crews," see Aug. 20, National Archives, Washington, D.C.; *Chicago Tribune*, Aug. 21, 1899.

11. Boyer, *Strange Adventures*, p. 57; Mansfield, *History of Great Lakes*, p. 723-4; U.S. Coast Guard, "Marine Casualties on the Great Lakes, 1863-73," Record Group 26, National Archives, Washington, D.C.

12. Canada, Air Services, "Accident Report," report 040902; idem, "Briefs," report 040902.

13. Canada, Air Services, serial 826.

14. Joseph Allen Hynek, *The UFO Experience: A Scientific Inquiry* (New York: Ballantine Books, 1974) p. 155.

15. George H. Seidlein, NTSB, "Factual," CHI 72-A-C036; Robert J. Hordon, "Specialist's Factual Report," CHI 72-A-C036 (confidential); Michael L. Marx, "Metallurgist's Factual Report," Metallurgical Laboratory Report No. 72-27 (confidential).

16. Canada, Air Services, "Accident Report," report 00090.

17. Robert L. Oelker, NTSB, "Factual"; U.S. Coast Guard record of search and rescue, "Cessna N2347U Missing," case 256-66, U.S. Coast Guard Headquarters, Washington, D.C. (also available from NTSB; see note 1, Chapter One).

18. CAB, "Briefs," docket 2-2259.

19. Canada, Air Services, "Accident Report," serial 55-F7.

20. See note 5, Chapter Two.

21. Canada, Air Services, "Accident Report," serial F-270.

22. *Chicago Tribune*, Aug. 28, 1953.

Chapter Three

1. *Chicago Tribune*, June 25, 1950.

2. Idem, Feb. 6, 1961.

3. Idem, Feb. 7, 1961; CAB, "Briefs," docket 2-4558.

4. Hynek, *UFO Experience*, pp. 41-2.

5. Air Traffic Controller Mike Parr, Chicago Air Route Traffic Control Center, Federal Aviation Administration, Department of Transportation, Aurora, Ill.

6. Hynek, *UFO Experience*, pp. 54-6.

7. *National Enquirer*, Aug. 3, 1976.

8. Ibid.

9. Ibid.

10. Donald Keyhoe, *Aliens from Space* (New York; Doubleday & Co., 1973), pp. 202-3.

11. Ibid., pp. 26-8.

12. J. Allen Hynek and Jacques Vallee, *The Edge of Reality* (Chicago: Henry Regnery Company, 1975), pp. 161-4.

Chapter Four

1. Boyer, *Great Stories*, pp. 179-80.

2. Ibid., pp. 180-1; Treasury Department, "Wreck Reports," Oct. 3, 1913, Record Group 26, National Archives, Washington, D.C.; Treasury Department, "Record of Marine Casualties,"

File No. 263, Record Group 26, National Archives, Washington, D.C.

3. *Cleveland Press*, Nov. 21, 1936.

4. Berlitz, *Bermuda Triangle*, p. 95.

5. *Chicago Tribune*, May 23, 1974.

6. Idem, May 14, 1962.

7. Mansfield, *History of Great Lakes*, p. 723.

8. U.S. Coast Guard, "Marine Board of Investigation; Tug *MV Sachem*, Foundering 59,000 ft. 036° True From Dunkirk Light, On Or About 18 December 1950, With Loss of Life," Coast Guard Headquarters, Washington, D.C.; *Cleveland Plain Dealer*, Dec. 19, 1950.

9. U.S. Coast Guard, "Marine Board, *Sachem*," p. 6.

10. Berlitz, *Bermuda Triangle*, pp. 89-90.

Chapter Five

1. Boyer, *Ghost Ships*, pp. 194-9; Dana Thomas Bowen, *Shipwrecks of the Lakes* (Cleveland: Freshwater Press, Inc., October 1952) pp. 313-23; *Cleveland Plain Dealer*, Dec. 3, 1942; idem, Dec. 4, 1942; idem, Oct. 10, 1969; idem, Dec. 8, 1942; idem, Jan. 27, 1944.

2. Ibid.

3. See note 5, Chapter Two.

4. Ibid.

5. Boyer, *Great Stories*, pp. 97-109; *Chicago American*, Dec. 21, 1917; idem, Aug. 20, 1919.

6. CAB, "Briefs," docket 2-4784.

7. Boyer, *Ghost Ships*, pp. 238-45.

8. CAB, "Accident Investigation Report: United Airlines, Inc., and American Airlines, Inc., Over Michigan City, Indiana—August 26, 1953," docket 1-0067; *Chicago Tribune*, Aug. 27, 1953; idem, Aug. 28, 1953.

9. Ibid.

10. NTSB, "Briefs," docket 1-0005; *Chicago Tribune*, June 30, 1972.

11. Ibid. (This citation involves a separate accident brief with the same designation as that cited above. The two briefs are filed next to each other. This was a midair collision and file numbers are assigned one to each accident, though there is a separate brief for each airplane.)

12. CAB, "Briefs," 1-0015; Fred G. Powell, CAB, "Factual."

13. Bowen, *Shipwrecks*, p. 229-33; Ratigan, *Shipwrecks Survivals*, pp. 255-6; *Chicago Tribune*, Oct. 13, 1907.

14. Rowley W. Murphy, "Ghosts of the Great Lakes," *Inland Seas*, Vol. 17, no. 2 (Summer 1961), pp. 94-96.

Chapter Six

1. NTSB, "Factual," CHI 68-A-53.
2. Hynek, *UFO Experience*, p. 133.
3. Ibid., p. 134.
4. CAB, "Briefs," docket 2-0153.
5. Canada, Air Services, "Accident Report," serial 985.
6. CAB, "Briefs," docket 2-1318.
7. NTSB, "Briefs," file 2-1016.
8. Canada, Air Services, "Accident Report," serial 56-F2.
9. NTSB, "Briefs," file 3-3961.
10. NTSB, "Briefs," file 3-0455; *Chicago Tribune*, April 6, 1970.
11. NTSB, "Briefs," file 3-2882.
12. NTSB, "Briefs," file 3-2818.
13. NTSB "Briefs," file 3-2504.
14. CAB, "Briefs," docket 2-1217, Appendix A.
15. CAB, "Briefs," docket 2-0220.

Chapter Seven

1. Canada, Air Services, "Accident Report," serial 51-F4.
2. CAB, "Briefs," docket 5-0005.
3. Boyer, *Strange Adventures*, pp. 74-107; *Chicago Tribune*, Nov. 13, 1940; idem, Nov. 14, 1940; *Cleveland Plain Dealer*, Nov. 19, 1940.
4. Ibid.
5. Jack G. Harrington, NTSB, "Factual," CHI-A-C008; NTSB, "Briefs," file 3-2958.
6. Canada, Air Services, "Summary."
7. Hynek, *UFO Experience*, p. 127.

Chapter Eight

1. NTSB, "Factual," MKC 73-A-K017; NTSB, "Briefs," file 3-2267.
2. CAB, "Briefs," docket 2-0861.
3. See note 1, Chapter Five.
4. CAB, "Accident Report," docket 2-0648; Robert D. Rudich, CAB, "Group Chairman's Analysis of Investigation, Air Traffic Control" (confidential); John J. Carroll, CAB, "Group Chairman's Analysis of Investigation, Human Factors Group" (confidential).

Chapter Nine

1. Berlitz, *Bermuda Triangle*, p. 113.
2. Ibid., p. 133.
3. Ibid., p. 126.
4. Edward J. McAvoy, NTSB, "Factual," CHI 68-A-81; Hubert McCaleb, NTSB, "Summary of Meteorological Factors Pertinent to the Accident Involving DeHavilland Dove, N999NJ, Chicago, Ill., March 8, 1968," CHI 68-A-81.
5. D. A. Nickerson, NTSB, "Factual," CHI 68-F-499.

Chapter Ten

1. NTSB, "Briefs," file 3-3317; *Chicago Tribune*, Nov. 11, 1969.
2. CAB, "Briefs," docket 2-0751.
3. J. O. Johnson, NTSB, "Factual," CHI 72-A-C039; NTSB, "Briefs," file 3-3832.
4. Edward J. McAvoy, NTSB, "Factual," CHI 71-A-C034; NTSB, "Briefs," file 3-2025.
5. NTSB, "Briefs," file 3-3543.
6. Robert B. Eberly, NTSB, "Factual," CHI 68-A-41.
7. CAB, "Briefs," docket 2-0918; *Chicago Tribune*, Dec. 2, 1964.
8. CAB, "Briefs," docket 1-0077; George J. Green, NTSB, "Analysis Report of Investigator in Charge" (confidential).

Chapter Eleven

1. Canada, Air Services, "Accident Report," report 030100; idem, "Briefs," 030100.
2. Joseph J. O'Connell, Jr., Oscar M. Laurel, John H. Reed, Louis M. Thayer and Francis H. McAdams, NTSB members, "Accident Report," file 1-0030; John J. Carroll, NTSB, "Analysis Report of Special Investigation Accident . . ." (confidential); I. W. Finch, NTSB, "Analysis Summary Report of Investigator in Charge" (confidential); Robert D. Rudich, NTSB, "Air Traffic Control Group Chairman's Analysis of Investigation" (confidential); Bruce G. Hoch, NTSB, "Operations Group Chairman's Analysis of Investigation" (confidential); Hubert McCaleb, NTSB, "Analysis of Meteorological Factors Pertinent to the Accident Involving . . ." (confidential); James T. Childs, NTSB, "Structures Investigation Report of Aircraft Accident Involving . . ." (confidential); Rudolph Kapustin, NTSB, "Report of Powerplant Investigation . . ." (confidential); Edmund B. Kraus, NTSB, "System's Group Chairman's Analysis of Investigation" (confidential); R. A. Roepe, NTSB, "Report of Human Factors Investigation" (confidential); Joseph Silva, NTSB, "Witness Group

Chairman's Analysis of Investigation" (confidential).

3. Jesse Watkins, Jr., "The Alpena Mystery," *Chicago Tribune*, Oct. 15, 1950 (Sunday Magazine); Boyer, *Ghost Ships*, pp. 176-88; Mansfield, *History of Great Lakes*, p. 734.

4. CAB, "Factual"; CAB, "Briefs," docket 2-0379.

5. Canada, Air Services, "Accident Report," serial 56-13.

6. Canada, Air Services, "Accident Report," serial 1039.

7. NTSB, "Briefs," file 3-3951; *Chicago Daily News*, Oct. 3, 1973; *Chicago Tribune*, Oct. 4, 1973.

8. George H. Seidlein, NTSB, "Factual," CHI 69-A-6.

9. Canada, Air Services, "Accident Report," serial 1134.

10. CAB, "Briefs," docket 2-4468.

11. NTSB, "Briefs," file 3-0121.

12. Jack G. Harrington, NTSB, "Factual," CHI 69-A-95; NTSB, "Briefs," file 3-3167.

13. NTSB, "Briefs," file 3-2534.

14. NTSB, "Briefs," file 3-3756.

15. NTSB, "Briefs," file 3-1328.

16. Canada, Air Services, "Accident Report," report 01041; idem, "Briefs," report 01074.

17. NTSB, "Briefs," file 3-0096.

18. E. D. Dreifus, CAB, "Factual," CHI 69-A-95; CAB, "Briefs," docket 3-3167.

Chapter Twelve

1. Mansfield, *History of Great Lakes*, p. 723.

2. CAB, "Briefs," docket 2-2311.

3. Boyer, *Ghost Ships*, pp. 144-71; *Chicago Record Herald*, Dec. 13, 1909.

Chapter Thirteen

1. David W. Kress, FAA, "Factual."

2. Ross Rizley, Joseph P. Adams, Josh Lee, Chan Gurney and Harmar D. Denny, CAB members, "Accident Investigation Report," file 1-0081.

3. *National Enquirer*, Aug. 19, 1976; Hynek, *UFO Experience*, pp. 178-85.

4. Canada, Air Services, "Accident Report," serial 4024.

5. Canada, Air Services, "Accident Report," serial F-411.

6. Canada, Air Services, "Accident Report," serial 2016.

Chapter Fourteen

1. Boyer, *Ghost Ships*, pp. 212-24; Ratigan, *Shipwrecks Survivals*, pp. 100-2.

2. Boyer, *Ghost Ships*, pp. 265-75; *Chicago Tribune*, Sept. 7, 1930.

3. Boyer, *True Tales of the Great Lakes* (New York: Dodd, Mead & Company 1971), pp. 266-302; Ratigan, *Shipwrecks Survivals*, pp. 99-136; *Annual Report United States Life-Saving Service*, 1914, Record Group 26, National Archives, Washington, D.C.

4. Boyer, *Strange Adventures*, pp. 225-7.

5. Boyer, *Ghost Ships*, pp. 126-43.

Chapter Fifteen

1. Boyer, *Ghost Ships*, pp. 126-43.

2. Boyer, *Great Stories*, p. 182-3.

3. Ibid.

4. Ibid.

5. Ibid., pp. 83-96.

6. Boyer, *Ghost Ships*, pp. 28-39; Bowen, *Shipwrecks*, pp. 250-3; U.S. Treasury Department, "Wreck Report," 1914, no. 70, Record Group 26, National Archives, Washington, D.C.; U.S. Life Saving Service, "Record of Marine Casualties," file 1370, Record Group 26, National Archives, Washington, D.C.

7. George H. Seidlein, NTSB, "Factual."

8. Canada, Air Services, "Accident Report," serial 52-51.

9. Robert L. Oelker, NTSB, "Factual."

10. George H. Seidlein, "Factual," CHI 70-A-27; NTSB, "Briefs," file 3-3766; *Chicago Tribune*, Nov. 7, 1969.

11. NTSB, "Briefs," file 3-1082.

12. George J. Green, NTSB, "Factual," CHI 73-A-C054; NTSB, "Briefs," file 3-3762.

13. Jack G. Harrington, NTSB, "Factual," CHI 73-A-C052; NTSB, "Briefs," file 3-3364.

14. Noel D. Lawson, CAB, "Factual," CHI 65-A-83; CAB, "Briefs," docket 2-1042; *Chicago Daily News*, Mar. 29, 1965.

15. Noel D. Lawson, CAB, "Factual"; Kenneth M. Kirton, Civil Air Patrol, "Statement" (on search).

16. NTSB, "Factual," CHI 69-A-97.

17. Daniel C. Sayres, NTSB, "Factual"; NTSB, "Briefs," file 3-2040.

18. NTSB, "Briefs," file 3-0582; *Cleveland Plain Dealer*, Mar. 22, 1973; idem, Mar. 23, 1973; idem, Mar. 26, 1973.

19. *Cleveland Plain Dealer*, Apr. 22, 1973; personal interview, Spencer Hardy, airport manager, Livingston County Airport, Howell, Mich. (No official government accident report on this presumed crash could be found in NTSB records. Consequently there is no registration number reported for the aircraft.)

20. Mansfield, *History of Great Lakes*, p. 640.

21. Dana Thomas Bowen, *Memories of the Lakes* (Cleveland: Freshwater Press, Inc., 1969) p. 78.

22. Jack G. Harrington, CAB, "Factual," CHI 66-A-75; idem, "Supplemental to Analysis Report," CHI 66-A-77 (confidential).

23. See note 5, Chapter Two.
24. See note 5, Chapter Two.
25. *National Enquirer*, Aug. 17, 1976.
26. Canada, Air Services, "Accident Report," serial F-185.

Chapter Sixteen

1. Canada, Air Services, "Accident Report," serial 675.
2. Ratigan, *Shipwrecks Survivals*, pp. 131-6; Boyer, *True Tales*, pp. 268-95.
3. Ibid.
4. Ibid.
5. Boyer, *Strange Adventures*, pp. 223-5; *Cleveland Press*, Apr. 29, 1937.
6. Mansfield, *History of Great Lakes*, p. 614; Boyer, *Strange Adventures*, p. 68.

INDEX